SOCCER FACTS

AND

TRIVIA

SOCCER FACTS

AND

TRIVIA

Geoff Tibballs

p

This is a Parragon Book
This edition published in 2001

Parragon
Queen Street House
4 Queen Street
Bath BA1 1HE, UK

Produced by Magpie Books, an imprint of
Constable & Robinson Ltd, London

ISBN 0-75254-731-3

A copy of the British Library Cataloguing-in-Publication Data
is available from the British Library

Printed and bound in the EC

ACKNOWLEDGEMENTS
Illustrations courtesy of Slatter-Anderson, London

CONTENTS

1

FIRST THINGS FIRST

1900 2000

SCORER INCOGNITO

The first goal in an FA Cup Final was scored by a man using an alias. M.P. Betts scored the only goal of the game for Wanderers against Royal Engineers in 1872 but he actually played under the name of A.H. Chequer. This was because he had been a member of the Harrow Chequers team which had scratched to Wanderers in the first round.

HONOURS EVEN

England and Scotland met in Glasgow for their first official international on 30 November 1872. The game ended 0–0.

ALEXANDER THE GREAT

The first player to score in successive FA Cup Finals was

Alexander Bonsor of Old Etonians who netted against Royal Engineers in 1875 and The Wanderers in 1876.

LIGHTING-UP TIME

The first floodlit match took place at Bramall Lane, Sheffield, in 1878 before a crowd of 20,000. But another early experiment was less successful. At Chorley, Lancashire, a crowd of 8000 went home disappointed after waiting two hours in torrential rain because nobody could switch on the lights.

FIRST GOAL

The first player to score a goal in the Football League was Gordon of Preston who netted on the opening day of the 1888–9 season.

HAT-TRICK HERO

The first player to score a Football League hat-trick was Walter Tait of Burnley who, on 8 September 1888, bagged three goals in his team's 4–3 victory over Bolton.

BIRTH OF THE PENALTY

The penalty kick was introduced in the Football League in the 1891–2 season and the first to be awarded was in the Wolves v Accrington match on 14 September 1891. Wolves' John Heath converted the kick to help his team to a 5–0 win.

NET GAIN

The goal as we now know it was born in 1891 with the introduction of nets. They were first used in a representative match between the North and the South. Crossbars had replaced tape as part of the goal frame 16 years earlier.

SOUTH AMERICAN KICK-OFF

In the first international to be played outside Britain, Argentina triumphed 3–2 in Uruguay in 1901.

THOUSAND UP

Aston Villa became the first club to score 1000 Football League goals when they reached that milestone in 1903–4 after only 450 matches.

OVERSEAS TRAILBLAZER

The first foreign player to turn out in the Football League was as long ago as season 1908–9 when a German, Max Seeburg, played for Spurs.

ROYAL VISITOR

King George V became the first reigning monarch to attend an FA Cup Final when he watched Burnley defeat Liverpool 1–0 in 1914.

HAPPY JACK

The first player to score in an FA Cup Final at Wembley was David Jack of Bolton Wanderers in 1923.

HELD BY BELGIANS

In Antwerp on 1 November 1923, Belgium became the first non-British team to avoid defeat by England. The game ended in a 2–2 draw.

CORNER EXPERT

Following the introduction of a new law which allowed players to score direct from a corner, Huddersfield Town's Billy Smith became the first player to score a League goal direct from a corner when he curled in a flag-kick against Arsenal on 11 October 1924.

ON AIR

The first Football League match to be broadcast on the radio was the Division One game between Arsenal and

Sheffield United on 22 January 1927. It ended in a 1–1 draw.

THE NUMBERS GAME

The first teams to wear numbered shirts in the Football League were Arsenal at Sheffield Wednesday and Chelsea at home to Swansea, both on 25 August 1928.

SCORING SPREE

The first 6–6 draw in the Football League took place between Leicester and Arsenal on 21 April 1930.

JUST CAPITAL!

In 1931, Arsenal became the first London club to win the League Championship.

ALBION'S DOUBLE

Also in 1931, West Bromwich Albion achieved the feat of winning the FA Cup and promotion to Division One in the same season – the first club to do so.

BORE DRAW

The first Football League match to be completed without a corner being awarded was the game between

Newcastle and Portsmouth on 5 December 1931. Not surprisingly, it finished in a goalless draw.

LIONS GO CLOSE

Millwall became the first Third Division side to reach the semi-finals of the FA Cup. They were narrowly beaten 2–1 by Sunderland.

WEMBLEY DATE

The first FA Cup Final to be televised was the 1937 final between Sunderland and Preston North End.

BONNIE FOR CLYDE

The first overseas player to score in a Scottish FA Cup Final was South African Dougie Wallace for Clyde against Motherwell in 1939. His goal helped Clyde to a 4–0 triumph.

FIRST WEMBLEY DISMISSAL

Yugoslavia's Boris Stankovic became the first player to be sent off at Wembley when he received his marching orders against Sweden in the 1948 Olympic Games.

OUR DARKEST HOUR

On 25 November 1953, Hungary's sensational 6–3 victory made them the first non-British team to defeat England at Wembley.

SCOTTISH INVASION

In 1955, Accrington Stanley fielded a team entirely composed of Scottish players – the first Football League club to do so.

JOHNSTONE AT THE DOUBLE

Bobby Johnstone of Manchester City became the first player to score in successive FA Cup Finals at Wembley when he scored against Newcastle United in 1955 and Birmingham City in 1956.

FLOODLIT CUP

The first FA Cup match to be played under floodlights was a 1955 preliminary round tie between Kidderminster Harriers and Brierley Hill Alliance. The first floodlit Football League game took place on 22 February 1956 between Portsmouth and Newcastle United.

BAREFOOT IN THE PARK

Wycombe Wanderers were the first British team to entertain a Ugandan touring side. In 1956 Wanderers defeated their barefoot opponents 10–1 at Loakes Park in front of a midweek crowd of 7450.

A WARM WELCOME

In 1958, Everton were the first British club to install undersoil heating.

OLD PALS' REUNION

Oldham Athletic and Bradford Park Avenue became the first teams to meet each other in Divisions One, Two, Three and Four of the Football League when they faced each other in a Fourth Division fixture in 1958.

ROUSE ROASTED

Crystal Palace's Welsh goalkeeper Vic Rouse became the first Fourth Division player to be picked for his country when he was chosen to play against Northern Ireland in 1959. The Welsh lost 4–1 and Rouse was never selected again.

LIVE AND KICKING

The first Football League match to be televised live was the Division One game between Blackpool and Bolton on 9 September 1960. It was intended to mark the start of regular Friday night TV soccer but the match, which Bolton won 1–0, was so dull that plans to screen future games were scrapped.

THE FIRST STRAW

In 1960, Ray Straw of Derby County and Coventry City became the first footballer to have played in all six divisions of the Football League (One, Two, Three, Four, Third (North) and Third (South)).

FIRST TO TREBLE

Aston Villa became the first club to win all three major English trophies when they defeated Rotherham United 3–2 on aggregate to lift the inaugural Football League Cup in 1961.

OH NO, IT'S NOT!

Danny Blanchflower of Spurs and Northern Ireland became the first person to refuse to be the subject of TV's *This Is Your Life* when he rejected Eamonn Andrews and his Big Red Book live on BBC on 30 April 1961.

HAYNES HITS THE JACKPOT

In 1961, Fulham's Johnny Haynes became the first British footballer to earn £100 a week.

BEES SPREAD THEIR WINGS

In the course of their Fourth Division campaign of 1962–3, Brentford became the first club to have played against the remaining 91 clubs in Football League membership at the time.

PANEL DEBUT

The first pools panel met on 26 January 1963 to decide for the benefit of the Football Pools on results of matches which had failed to beat the big freeze. The first panel was comprised solely of former players – Ted Drake, Tom Finney, Tommy Lawton and George Young.

BRADFORD BUDDIES

In season 1963–4, Bradford City and Bradford Park Avenue became the first two teams from the same city to meet each other in four divisions of the Football League.

FIRST *MOTD*

The first game to be shown on *Match of the Day* was the Division One match between Liverpool and Arsenal on 22 August 1964. Liverpool won 3–2 and commentator Kenneth Wolstenholme remembers it for a cat holding up play by running across the Liverpool goalmouth. *Match of the Day* began on the new BBC2 channel which at the time was only available in the London area. So there were almost as many spectators at Anfield that day as there were viewers of the programme. For the record, the second edition of *Match of the Day* saw Chelsea beat Sunderland 3–1.

SUPERSUB

Charlton's Keith Peacock became the first substitute to be used in the Football League when he came on during the Second Division game against Bolton on 21 August 1965.

CLOSED-CIRCUIT GAME

Coventry City staged the first closed-circuit TV match on 6 October 1965. A crowd of over 10,000 watched the 2–1 win at Cardiff on four large screens at Highfield Road.

SUBSTITUTE'S HAT-TRICK

Birmingham City's Geoff Vowden was the first

substitute to score a Football League hat-trick. He netted three after coming on against Huddersfield Town in a Division Two game on 7 September 1968.

COLOURFUL REDS

The first TV game in colour was between Liverpool and West Ham on 15 November 1969.

KELLY'S EYE IN

Eddie Kelly became the first substitute to score in an FA Cup Final when he notched Arsenal's equaliser in the 1971 clash with Liverpool.

DEREK'S DELIGHT

The 86th minute equaliser by Rangers' Derek Johnstone against Celtic in 1971 made him the first substitute to score in the Scottish FA Cup Final.

SUNDAY START

The first Football League game to take place on a Sunday was the Second Division match between Millwall and Fulham on 20 January 1974. Millwall's Brian Clark scored the only goal of the game.

GOD-FEARING

The first player to refuse to play in a Football League game on a Sunday was Swindon Town keeper Jimmy Allan in 1974. With Sunday morning and afternoon matches being introduced to cope with a national power crisis, Swindon announced that they would be playing their Second Division match with Bolton on a Sunday. But Allan refused to play on religious grounds.

TREAD CAREFULLY

In 1976, Kettering Town became the first English club to carry shirt sponsorship when their players took to the field with "Kettering Tyres" emblazoned across their chests.

ARE YOU SITTING COMFORTABLY?

By doing away with the terraces at Pittodrie in 1978, Aberdeen were the first British club to provide all-seater accommodation.

BLACK BREAKTHROUGH

On 29 November 1978, Viv Anderson became the first black player to appear for England in a full international – against Czechoslovakia.

THE AGE OF PLASTIC

Queens Park Rangers staged the first Football League game on artificial turf when they rolled out the plastic to play Luton on 1 September 1981. Coincidentally, Luton became the second club to install an artificial pitch.

THREE-POINT WIN

In 1981, the Football League increased the number of points for a win to three instead of two.

LIVERPOOL'S TREBLE

Liverpool became the first English club to do a treble when, in 1984, they won the League, the League Cup and the European Champions' Cup.

MORAN'S MISERY

Kevin Moran of Manchester United achieved the un-enviable distinction of being the first player to be sent off in an FA Cup Final when he was dismissed by referee Peter Willis in the 1985 final with Everton.

GROUND SHARE SCHEME

In 1985, Crystal Palace and Charlton were the first

clubs to share a ground (Palace's Selhurst Park) in the history of the Football League.

LERBY AT THE DOUBLE

On 13 November 1985, Soren Lerby became the first player to play in two different countries on the same day. After appearing for Bayern Munich in Germany, he turned out in an international for Denmark in Copenhagen.

KEPT AROUND

In 1986–7, goalkeeper Eric Nixon became the first player to appear in all four divisions of the Football League in one season. In the First Division, he played five games for Manchester City and four for Southampton; in the Second Division, he made three appearances for Bradford City; in the Third Division he turned out 16 times for Carlisle United; and in the Fourth Division he kept goal on 16 occasions for Wolves.

THE FIRST PLAY-OFFS

In 1987, play-off matches were introduced to decide the final promotion and relegation places in the Football League. The first teams to be promoted as a result of the play-offs were Swindon Town (into Division Two) and Aldershot (into Division Three). Charlton preserved their First Division status by defeating Leeds. Those first play-offs also saw Sunderland slip into Division

Three and Bolton drop into Division Four, both for the first time in their history.

LINCOLN'S LAPSE

Also in 1987, Lincoln City became the first team to be relegated from the Football League to the Conference.

TWIN TRIP TO TWIN TOWERS

Nottingham Forest became the first club to reach two Wembley finals in the same season when they reached the finals of the League Cup and the Simod Cup in 1989.

ONCE A CATHOLIC . . .

In July 1989, Rangers signed their first Catholic player – ex-Celtic striker Mo Johnston. Some Ibrox fans burnt their season tickets in protest.

A HINT OF THE EAST

On 19 December 1990, Matthias Sammer became the first East German to play for the new united Germany when he took the field against Switzerland in Stuttgart.

CHAMPIONS' CHOKER

By defeating Arsenal 2–1 in a fourth round FA Cup tie on 4 January 1992, Wrexham became the first team finishing bottom of the Football League the previous season to knock out the reigning champions.

BACK-PASS RULE

The new back-pass rule was introduced in 1992 whereby a goalkeeper is not allowed to handle a ball kicked to him by a team-mate.

NEW LEAGUE FORMAT

The FA Carling Premiership was created for the 1992–3 season, supported by three divisions of the Football League.

REPEAT FINALS

In 1993, Arsenal became the first team to win the FA Cup and the League Cup in the same season. In both finals, their victims were Sheffield Wednesday. It was also the first time that the same two teams had met in both major domestic finals in one year.

GOLDEN GOAL

The first Wembley match to be decided by a golden goal was the 1995 Auto Windscreens Shield Final. Paul Tait scored in the 103rd minute to give Birmingham City victory over Carlisle.

DREAM DEBUT

Michael Ricketts scored with his first touch of the ball on his League debut after coming on as a substitute for Walsall against Brighton in May 1996.

CZECHS BOUNCED OUT

Euro 96 became the first major international competition to be decided by a golden goal when Germany's Oliver Bierhoff scored the winner in the 95th minute of the final against the Czech Republic.

RUUD AWAKENING

Ruud Gullit became the first foreign manager to lift the FA Cup when he led Chelsea to victory in 1997.

NUMBER ONE AND NUMBER TWO

Fan Zhiyi and Sun Jihai became the first Chinese

players in England when they signed for Crystal Palace on 14 August 1998.

ARSENE'S TITLE

Arsene Wenger went down in the records as the first foreign manager to win the Football League Championship when he led Arsenal to the Premiership title in 1998.

WOE, WOE AND THRICE WOE!

When John Barnes came on as a substitute for Newcastle during their 1998 FA Cup Final defeat to Arsenal, he became the first player to lose Wembley FA Cup Finals with three different clubs. He had previously tasted defeat at the Twin Towers with Watford in 1984 and with Liverpool in 1988 and 1996.

UNITED GLORY

In 1999, Manchester United became the first English club to do the supreme treble of League, FA Cup and UEFA Champions' League.

2

CLUB CALL

BECKHAM ON LOAN

David Beckham was sent on a month's loan to Third Division Preston North End in March 1995. He started four games at Deepdale, plus one as substitute, and scored twice – in a 2–2 draw at home to Doncaster on 4 March and in the 3–2 victory over Fulham the following week. During his stay, Preston won three (including a 5–0 hammering of Bury) and drew two, and young Beckham was named man-of-the-match on three occasions. He played in two away games – at Exeter and Lincoln. The Exeter match, on a Tuesday night, was watched by a crowd of just 2057 – a far cry from the heady days of Old Trafford.

CASH-STRAPPED

In an effort to save money, hard-up Portsmouth cancelled their weekly order of new jockstraps in 1999. Instead of buying new ones each week – £112 for 14 –

administrator Tom Burton ordered the club to wash the old ones.

PARTY TIME

In a bid to boost the attendance at Ashton Gate for the match with West Ham in 1976, Bristol City staged a chimps tea-party before kick-off.

DEVON TOURISTS

The first game ever to be played by a Brazilian national XI was against . . . Exeter City. It took place in the summer of 1914 when Exeter became the first English club to go on an extensive tour of South America. They played eight matches in Argentina and Brazil and, remarkably, lost only once.

POSTS REMOVED

In the summer of 1986 bailiffs removed the goalposts from Hartlepool's Victoria Ground to pay off the club debts.

HOME FROM HOME

Sheffield United's hopes of gaining promotion to the First Division in 1938–9 were in danger of being scuppered by their poor home form. So manager Ted

Davison decided to treat their last three home matches as away games. On each Saturday morning before the final three home games, the players were driven by bus from Sheffield to Derbyshire where they had lunch. Then they returned to the city for the match. The psychology worked: United won two and drew one of those vital games to snatch promotion at the expense of neighbours Sheffield Wednesday.

DALEY ON THE BENCH

Former Olympic decathlon champion Daley Thompson once trained with Mansfield Town, but never made it beyond the substitutes' bench.

FAMOUS NAMES

Liverpool used to have a full-back called Tommy Cooper, and Wolves once had a goalkeeper by the name of Charlie Chaplin. And in the 1950s Darlington signed a right-winger called Baden Powell. Presumably he was spotted by the club scout.

SLEEPING GIANTS

With a population of over 270,000, Hull is the largest city in England never to have hosted top-flight football.

RUST'S REWARD

After letting in nine goals on his debut – against Peterborough United in 1998 – Barnet goalkeeper Nicky Rust was rewarded with a two-year contract. "He did pretty well in tricky conditions," said Barnet boss John Still.

THE UNHAPPY EIGHT

Eight of the current English League clubs have never played at Wembley – Exeter City, Halifax Town, Hartlepool United, Hull City, Lincoln City, Rochdale, Walsall and Wrexham. Barnsley removed their name from the list in the First Division play-off final in May 2000 . . . even though it wasn't a happy ending for the Tykes.

THE MIGHTY QUINN

In 1995–6, Reading gained their first victory over West Bromwich Albion for 67 years . . . despite striker Jimmy Quinn having to play in goal for the second half.

HERO TO ZERO

Playing at Sunderland on 21 November 1998, Barnsley striker Ashley Ward scored, missed a penalty and was sent off – all in the space of five minutes.

A TEAM OF TYKES

In the days before the influx of foreign players, teams often fielded a large proportion of local lads. Rotherham United's 1951–2 line-up regularly contained ten Yorkshiremen, the only exception being wing-half Colin Rawson who was born over the border in north Nottinghamshire.

COSTLY COUNTY

In December 1970 Stockport County were the most expensive team to watch in the Football League. The minimum cost of admission to Edgeley Park rose to 10 shillings after chairman Predrag Lukic said the directors couldn't afford to put any more money into the club.

SCANT REWARD

Despite being one of the all-time greats, the only club prize which Sir Tom Finney won in his playing career was a Second Division champions' medal with Preston in 1951. After that, it was a case of so near but yet so far. In 1953 Preston finished runners-up in the First Division (beaten by Arsenal on goal average) and the following year they narrowly lost 2–3 to West Bromwich Albion in the FA Cup Final after leading 2–1. Four years later they again had to settle for the runners-up spot in the First Division, this time behind Wolves.

THE FIRST CITY

The first "City" in the Football League were Lincoln who joined in 1892. Although Stoke had been one of the founder members four years earlier, they didn't add "City" to their name until later.

GENEROUS GESTURE

After Third Division leaders Cardiff City had been held 1–1 by cash-strapped Barnet at Ninian Park in March 1993, Cardiff chairman Rick Wright handed the visiting players (who hadn't been paid for weeks) £1000 for a drink and a meal on the way home. Two days later, Barnet chairman Stan Flashman threatened to fine his players two weeks' wages for complaining about not being paid!

BUSY SEASON

Stockport County played no fewer than 67 games in the course of the 1996–7 season.

SWIFTS' SIT-IN

On 29 December 1893 Walsall Town Swifts staged a sit-down protest in their dressing-room prior to a Second Division fixture against Newcastle, claiming that they had not been paid expenses. Eventually club officials persuaded them to play the match but, after 70 minutes and with Newcastle leading 3–2, bad light caused the game to be abandoned. However, the result was allowed to stand.

LOYALTIES DIVIDED

Injury-hit Manchester City fielded John Burridge as an emergency goalkeeper against Newcastle United on 29 April 1995 . . . even though Burridge was employed at the time as goalkeeping coach to Newcastle.

DID HE NOT LIKE THAT!

When Watford thrashed Grimsby Town 7–1 at Vicarage Road in 1967, Graham Taylor was Grimsby's left-back.

THE STRIFE OF BRIAN

Exeter City manager Brian Godfrey was so appalled with his team's display during a 5–1 defeat at Millwall in a Sunday game in 1984 that as punishment he kept his players in London overnight to play Millwall's reserves the next day. The exercise offered little comfort since Exeter even managed to lose to the Lions' second string 1–0.

MINI MARVEL

As a player with Leeds United in the mid-1970s, striker

Duncan McKenzie's party piece in training used to be vaulting over a Mini car.

A ONE-OFF

Blackpool won only one First Division game at Bloomfield Road in 1966–7, but it was one to remember. For they thrashed Newcastle United 6–0.

11-GOAL DEBUT

Barnet's first game in the Football League saw them lose 4–7 at home to Crewe Alexandra on 17 August 1991.

THE CREWE CHAIN

After being beaten 4–3 at home by Crewe Alexandra on 30 November 1990, Cambridge United embarked on a club record run of 16 League and Cup games without defeat. The run ended on 1 March when they lost 3–1 . . . at Crewe. Seven years earlier, Cambridge had broken an unwanted record which had stood for 27 years by going 31 games without a win. The previous holders were . . . Crewe.

SCORING SUBS

When Barnet beat Torquay United 5–4 in the Third

Division on 28 December 1993, it was the first time all four substitutes had scored in a Football League match.

TV JINX

When Charlton beat West Bromwich Albion in front of the cameras on 5 February 1995, it was their first victory on live television since the 1947 FA Cup Final.

A GAME OF THREE HALVES

A First Division game between Sunderland and Derby County on 1 September 1884 was played over three periods of 45 minutes. With no sign of the referee at kick-off time, one of the linesmen took charge. At half-time Sunderland led 3–0 but then the referee appeared and demanded that the match be started all over again. So the teams proceeded to play another 90 minutes, during which time Sunderland added eight more goals. But the first three of their 11 – scored in the half that never was – were expunged from the records.

NOT-SO-ABLE SEAMAN

David Seaman made an inauspicious start to his League career. Rejected by Leeds, he ended up at Peterborough United before being transferred to Birmingham City where, in 1986, he was a member of the Blues' team beaten 2–1 at St Andrews by Altrincham in an FA Cup third round tie.

OGGY'S FINEST HOUR

Coventry City goalkeeper Steve Ogrizovic, who retired at the end of last season, once clean bowled the great Viv Richards while playing cricket for Shropshire in the NatWest Trophy against Somerset.

WRONG PRIORITIES

When Third Division strugglers Workington increased their number of board members to 13 in October 1966, they had more directors than full-time players.

SWEET AND SOUR

Arsenal's record victory and record defeat both came against the same club – Loughborough Town. In 1896, the Gunners crashed 8–0 at Loughborough in a Second Division game, but four years later they gained revenge by putting 12 past the Midlands team without reply.

McNAMARA'S BAND

Right-winger Tony McNamara played in all four divisions of the Football League within 12 months. On 12 October 1957 he made his final appearance for Everton in Division One before moving across Stanley Park to play for Second Division Liverpool. He then moved on to Fourth Division Crewe, and on 27 September 1958 made his debut for Bury in Division Three.

STEADY LIONS

In three successive seasons between 1929 and 1931, Millwall finished 14th in Division Two with 39 points.

LATE SUB

Following the introduction of the substitute rule at the start of the 1965–6 season, Notts County were the last Football League club to use a substitute in an actual game. They waited until 5 February 1966 before bringing on Dennis Shiels in place of Brian Bates during the match with Lincoln City.

UNLUCKY MASCOT

Arsenal's lucky mascot is a dray horse which was killed in an accident while Highbury was being built and was buried under what became the North Bank.

CAR WASH

The players at cash-strapped Mansfield washed cars at £3 a time at a local shopping centre to raise enough money to pay for an overnight stay before their Third Division promotion clash at Torquay on Easter Monday 1999. They raised some £800 – sufficient to prevent them having to make a 4 a.m. start from Nottingham-shire to the West Country. They returned home with a 0–0 draw.

THE JONES BOYS

During a 3–2 victory over Aldershot on New Year's Day 1966, Chester lost both their full-backs – Ray Jones and Bryn Jones – with broken left legs.

UNBROKEN MEMBERSHIP

Barnsley spent the first 33 years of their Football League membership (1899–1932) in Division Two. The tedium was finally broken when they were relegated – on goal average after finishing level on points with Port Vale – to the Third Division (North).

A COMPACT DIVISION

When Arsenal won the League Championship in 1938, they finished with only 16 more points than the bottom club, West Bromwich Albion.

INJURY FREE

Tranmere Rovers fielded an unchanged team for the first 28 matches of the 1977–8 season in Division Three. It was not until the home match with Hereford United on 20 January 1978 that Rovers made their first change of the season.

BLUE WAS THE COLOUR

By the end of a wet and windswept match at Blackpool on 31 October 1931, five Chelsea players were so cold that they left the pitch for the comparative warmth of the dressing-room long before the final whistle. Blackpool won 4–0. On the same day, at Blackburn, two of the home side and three Sheffield United players were treated for exposure. The referee also collapsed from the cold and had to be replaced by one of the linesmen.

HIS BOTTLE WENT

A 1954 game between Luton Town and Stoke City was stopped while the referee asked a boy in the crowd to hide a bottle of orange juice because the bright sunshine was reflecting from the bottle into the players' eyes.

BREAKING THE ICE

Without a win in Division Three for nearly three months, Sheffield Wednesday players were ordered by assistant manager Tony Toms to spend a night in January 1976 on bleak Broomhead Moor to build up camaraderie. It turned out to be one of the coldest nights of the winter with a hard frost and a biting wind. At the end of the season, Wednesday stayed up by a single point.

CHURCH CLASH

Everton once agreed to put back the kick-off because a local vicar, a devout Evertonian, didn't want the match to clash with his Harvest Festival service.

JOKE BACKFIRED

For an April Fool's Day joke in 1995, Torquay United took to the field against Hereford United in the colours of local rivals Exeter City. The change seemed to baffle their own players more than Hereford's who returned home with a surprise 1–0 victory.

PELE AT PLYMOUTH

The great Pele once scored at Home Park, Plymouth. He was a member of the Santos team which lost 3–2 at Plymouth in a friendly in 1973.

DONNY DEBUT

Doncaster Rovers' first game of any sort, in 1879, was against the Yorkshire Institution for the Deaf!

SUPREME OPTIMISTS

Despite having crashed 10–0 to Liverpool at Anfield in the first leg of their League Cup tie in 1986, Fulham defiantly printed details in their programme of what would happen should the tie be all square at the end of 90 minutes in the second leg. The information proved superfluous as Liverpool won 3–2 for an aggregate victory of 13–2.

TEN NEW BOYS

The Rochdale team which played Carlisle in a Third Division (North) fixture on 27 August 1932 contained no fewer than ten men who were making their League debuts.

GILLS IN DEEP WATER

After missing their train from Euston, Gillingham had to charter a plane to have any hope of reaching Barrow in time for the scheduled 5.15 kick-off of their Fourth Division fixture on 9 October 1961. But despite the Gills' mad dash, the game kicked off late and eventually had to be abandoned after 75 minutes because of failing light, Barrow having no floodlights. Barrow, who were leading 7–0 at the time, were relieved when the League ruled that the scoreline should stand as a result. Gillingham were simply relieved that they didn't have to travel to Barrow again that season.

SPANISH HIGHS

Swansea beat Real Madrid 3–0 in 1927 during a close-season tour of Spain and Portugal. But they weren't the first club to defeat Real on home soil – Nelson had done so four years previously.

BEEFY'S BEST

England cricketer Ian Botham came on as a substitute for Scunthorpe against Bournemouth in March 1980.

A KNIGHT IN GOAL

Former FIFA President Sir Stanley Rous played a few games in goal for Exeter City Reserves in 1919 while studying at a nearby teacher training college.

COLOUR CLASH

Walsall were forced to change their shirts during the first half of a Coca-Cola Cup tie at Nottingham Forest in 1997 because they clashed with those of the linesmen.

SAINTS STUNNED

In 1980–1, after losing the first leg of their League Cup tie at Southampton 4–0 Watford could have been forgiven for thinking they were all but out of the competition. But they won the second leg at Vicarage Road 7–1 after extra time to go through 7–5.

OH DIA!

Acting on the apparent recommendation of George Weah, Southampton manager Graeme Souness gave 30-year-old Senegal striker Ali Dia a run-out in the Premiership. However, it was quickly apparent that Dia was not up to the mark and further investigations revealed that the call from Weah was a hoax. The Liberian international knew nothing about it. So Dia was shuffled off to somewhere nearer his standard – Gateshead.

BIN THE PINK

Struggling in the lower reaches of the Third Division in 1992–3, Torquay United decided to employ a little psychology by painting the away dressing-room at Plainmoor "sleepy pink". The idea was that the peaceful pastel shades would lull opponents into a state of tranquillity and drowsiness before taking the field. The plan was by no means an unqualified success and following another four home defeats in quick succession, Torquay decided to redecorate . . .

SILENCED!

In 1995, Swindon Town PA announcer Pete Lewis was sacked for criticising referee George Barber over the tannoy at half-time in the 1–0 defeat to Bolton at the County Ground. The irony was that Lewis himself was a local football referee.

STAN'S THE MAN

Birmingham City full-back Stan Lynn finished as the club's top League goalscorer in 1964–5. He scored ten times, eight from penalties.

THREE ORIGINALS

Only three clubs that were among the original 12 members of the Football League in 1888 were also in the first FA Carling Premiership season in 1992 – Aston Villa, Blackburn Rovers and Everton.

NOVEL SOLUTION

Arriving at Middlesbrough railway station in the late 1940s, the Bolton Wanderers entourage were horrified to discover that the players' shinguards had been left behind in Lancashire. So enterprising trainer Bill Ridding went to the local bookshop and bought 22 paperback romantic novels to act as temporary replacements.

NAMESAKE

On 7 September 1997, 18-year-old Clarke Carlisle scored an injury-time winner for Blackpool . . . against Carlisle.

RUSSIAN TOURISTS

West Bromwich Albion were the first British club to win a match in the Soviet Union. On a summer tour in 1957, they defeated Dynamo Tbilisi 3–0 and, for good measure, followed up with a 4–2 victory over CSKA Moscow.

AN UNWANTED AWARD

His own goal having secured promotion to the First Division for Nottingham Forest in 1977, grateful Forest supporters voted Millwall's Jon Moore their Player of the Year that evening.

SAM IN A HAZE

When Chelsea entertained Charlton on Christmas Day 1937, a search party had to be sent out on to the Stamford Bridge pitch to locate Charlton keeper Sam Bartram who was blissfully unaware that the game had been abandoned due to thick fog five minutes earlier.

JACKO'S VISIT

Singer Michael Jackson did a lap of honour around Craven Cottage in April 1999 before watching Fulham play Wigan in a Second Division game. Jackson, a guest of Fulham owner Mohamed Al Fayed, was obviously a good omen as Fulham won 2–0, but the match was anything but a thriller.

YORK TRAGEDY

The last player to die during a senior match in Britain was 25-year-old York City forward David Longhurst who was carried off two minutes before half-time in the Fourth Division game with Lincoln on 8 September 1990. It later emerged that he suffered from a rare heart condition. The match was abandoned.

FANGS VERY MUCH

Leicester striker Alan Smith lost three teeth during a 2–2 draw with Stoke in 1983. The missing molars were later found on the pitch by groundstaff and replaced in hospital.

LOCAL SUPPORT

With average gates of 13,000 from a town with a population of less than 100,000, Burnley can lay claim to being the best-supported club in Britain in 2000.

BAD TASTE

In 1990, the Football League banned Scarborough from wearing shirts advertising Black Death vodka on the grounds of dubious taste.

PHLEGMATIC

Usually laid-back Aston Villa striker Savo Milosevic was transfer-listed in 1998 after spitting at his own fans during a defeat at Blackburn.

3

GOALS, GOALS, GOALS

DRAMATIC FINALE

The most dramatic goal in the history of the Football League was that scored by Arsenal's Michael Thomas at Anfield with virtually the last kick of the 1989 season. Arsenal went into the match three points behind First Division leaders Liverpool and with an inferior goal difference of four. Alan Smith had given the Gunners the lead but as the match went into injury time, Liverpool were about to be crowned champions. But then Thomas burst through for the killer second goal which put the teams level on points and goal difference yet gave Arsenal the title by virtue of having scored more goals. By a twist of fate, Thomas later became a Liverpool player.

A RICH VEIN

Tom Jennings of Leeds United just couldn't stop scoring in the autumn of 1926. On 25 September he scored a hat-trick against Arsenal. In the next game, on 2 October, he scored four against Liverpool at Anfield and he completed his hat-trick of hat-tricks by netting three against Blackburn a week later. Despite his efforts, Leeds were relegated at the end of the season.

HOORAY, HENRY

His goal for Arsenal in the 3–3 draw with Sheffield Wednesday in May 2000 meant that Frenchman Thierry Henry had scored in seven successive Premiership matches. This equalled the record of Chelsea's Mark Stein, Ian Wright of Arsenal and Newcastle United's Alan Shearer.

FASTEST GOAL

Jim Fryatt of Bradford Park Avenue scored what is believed to be the fastest Football League goal on record when he claimed a goal after just four seconds of the match with Tranmere on 25 April 1964. League goals in six seconds have been scored by Aldershot's Albert Mundy (against Hartlepool on 25 October 1958), Newport County's Barrie Jones (against Torquay United on 31 March 1962) and Crystal Palace's Keith Smith (against Derby County on 12 December 1964).

SPURS CORNERED

In April 1924, Everton's Sam Chedgzoy exploited a loophole in the laws by taking a corner to himself and dribbling through the bemused Spurs defence before firing into the net. The rule regarding corner-kicks was subsequently amended to prevent a reoccurrence.

13 IN A ROW

Bill Prendergast of Chester holds the Football League record for consecutive scoring. He found the net in 13 successive games in 1938.

ROBBIE'S GOAL RUSH

Liverpool's Robbie Fowler scored a Premiership hat-trick in just four and a half minutes against Arsenal on 28 August 1994. But he was a sloth compared to Maglioni of Argentine club Independiente who scored three in 1 minute 50 seconds against Gimnasia de la Plata on 18 March 1973. The fastest Football League hat-trick was by Gillingham's Jimmy Scarth. He scored three in two minutes against Leyton Orient in a Third Division (South) match on 1 November 1952.

THE FABULOUS BAKER BOYS

In 1961, a year after St Mirren's Gerry Baker had set a post-war Scottish FA Cup record by smashing ten goals past Glasgow University, his brother nearly equalled the record by scoring nine times for Hibernian against Peebles Rovers.

BULLY FOR HIM

Steve Bull reached the 50-goal mark in two successive seasons for Wolves. In 1987–8, he scored 52 goals (including 34 in the League) and the following year he netted 50 (37 of them in the League).

GOODISON GOAL GLUT

Everton rattled in 33 goals in four successive home games in the autumn of 1931. They beat Sheffield Wednesday 9–3, Newcastle United 8–1, Chelsea 7–2 and Leicester City 9–2.

CHAMPAGNE CORK

Alan Cork scored in all four divisions of the Football League and the FA Premier League during his 18-year career with Wimbledon, Sheffield United and Fulham between 1977 and 1995.

SIX OUT OF SIX

When Ted Drake scored all seven of Arsenal's goals in

their 7–1 away win at Aston Villa on 14 December 1935, his first six goals came from his first six shots.

HARPER'S BIZARRE

Joe Harper of Hibernian scored a hat-trick in the 1975 Scottish League Cup Final yet still finished on the losing side. His team were beaten 6–3 by Celtic with Dixie Deans scoring a hat-trick for the Bhoys. The result brought back unhappy memories for Hibs. Three years earlier Celtic had trounced them 6–1 in the Scottish FA Cup Final . . . and on that occasion too Dixie Deans had scored a hat-trick.

BLY'S HALF-CENTURY

The last player to score 50 Football League goals in a season was Terry Bly who bagged 52 as Peterborough United swept to the Division Four title in 1960–1. Peterborough scored 134 goals that season – their first in the League.

GUNNAR SHOOTS 'EM DOWN

Coming on as a late substitute for Manchester United at Nottingham Forest in 1999, Ole Gunnar Solskjaer scored four times in 13 minutes to steer United to a resounding 8–1 victory.

BROAD SHOULDERED THE BURDEN

Demobbed from the army at the end of the First World War, Jimmy Broad walked into The Den and asked for a trial with Millwall. The Lions could hardly believe their luck. In season 1919–20, he netted 32 of their 52 League goals, the club's next highest scorer managing a paltry four.

BACK TO SCOTLAND

Ally McCoist may have been a big hit north of the border but he didn't exactly set the world alight in his two years with Sunderland. Having signed from St Johnstone for £300,000 in 1981, he went on to score just eight goals in 56 League games for the Wearsiders and was sold back to Scotland in 1983 for a cut-price £180,000.

THREE OF A KIND

When Manchester City beat Huddersfield 10–1 in a Second Division game on 7 November 1987, Tony Adcock, Paul Stewart and David White each scored hat-tricks.

HILL HATH NO FURY

In his playing days, Jimmy Hill once scored all five goals for Fulham in a 5–1 victory at Doncaster.

SUPERMAC

Bournemouth striker Ted MacDougall is the only player to have scored double hat-tricks on two occasions in the FA Cup. On 24 November 1970, he scored six times in the 8–1 thrashing of Oxford City, and on 20 November 1971 he netted nine in the 11–0 annihilation of Margate.

NO PLACE LIKE HOME

The first 19 of Wilf Grant's Second Division goals for Cardiff City in season 1951–2 were all scored at Ninian Park.

UNLIKELY HEROES

Due to an injury crisis, Hull City named their Northern Ireland goalkeeper Alan Fettis as an outfield substitute for the Second Division match with visiting Oxford United on 17 December 1994. Coming on near the end, he promptly netted the third goal in Hull's 3–1 victory. To prove it was no fluke, he repeated the feat in the final game of the season against Blackpool. Fettis was following in the footsteps of Luton Town keeper Tony Read who, due to injuries, found himself playing up front against Notts County on 20 November 1965. Read bagged three goals in a 5–1 win – the only time a recognised goalkeeper has scored a hat-trick in the Football League.

RECORD SCORE

The record score in a senior British match is Arbroath's 36–0 drubbing of Bon Accord in a Scottish Cup tie on 12 September 1885. Contemporary reports stated that Milne, the Arbroath goalkeeper, didn't have to touch the ball during the entire 90 minutes and spent most of the game smoking his pipe while sheltering from the rain under an umbrella. However, Bon Accord did have an excuse. The Scottish FA had sent out the invitation by mistake to Orion Cricket Club instead of Orion FC of Aberdeen. But the cricketers thought they'd have a go at football and changed their name to Bon Accord. They had to switch the tie to Arbroath because they had no pitch of their own and turned up for the tie without either shirts or boots. Incidentally, on the same day Dundee Harp hammered Aberdeen Rovers 35–0, also in the Scottish Cup.

SUPERTED

Ted Harston made a lively debut for Mansfield Town on 19 October 1935, rattling a hat-trick in the first seven minutes of the Third Division (North) game with Southport. But the day went downhill from there as Southport fought back for a 3–3 draw. The following year, in his first full season, Harston scored 55 League goals – a record for the division.

THE FLYING FINN

Danish striker Finn Dossing scored in 15 consecutive

Scottish First Division matches for Dundee United in 1964–5.

SPACED OUT

Frank Dudley's first three goals of the 1953–4 season were scored for three different clubs in three different divisions. His first was for Southampton against Watford in Division Three (South) on 19 August; his second was for Cardiff City against Charlton Athletic in a First Division match on 31 October; and his third was for Brentford against Oldham Athletic in Division Two on Christmas Day.

EIGHT ON THE MARK

When Liverpool thumped Crystal Palace 9–0 in a First Division match at Anfield on 12 September 1989, the goals were spread between no fewer than eight players – a Football League record. The eight were Steve Nicol (who scored twice), Steve McMahon, Ian Rush, Gary Gillespie, Peter Beardsley, John Aldridge, John Barnes and Glenn Hysen.

SIX IN TWO DAYS

Watford's Cliff Holton is the only player to have scored Football League hat-tricks on consecutive days. He scored three in the 4–2 win over Chester in a Fourth Division match on 15 April 1960, and the next day he scored three more in the 5–0 victory over Gateshead.

SHIFT IN FORTUNE

After going ten games without scoring a goal in 1976–7, Sunderland proceeded to score 17 in the next four.

SAINT ON SONG

The fastest hat-trick in Scotland was by Ian St John in his Motherwell days. Playing at Hibernian in a Scottish League Cup tie on 15 August 1959, the Saint struck three times in two and a half minutes to help Motherwell to a 3–1 win.

HOT-SHOT UNITED

Manchester United hold the record for the highest scores home and away in the Premiership. They crushed Ipswich Town 9–0 on 4 March 1995 at Old Trafford and humiliated Nottingham Forest 8–1 at the City Ground on 6 February 1999.

GOAL-MAD SATURDAY

The 44 Football League matches played on 1 February 1936 produced a staggering 209 goals – the most ever scored on one day. The highest-scoring division was Third (North) with 68 goals, results including Crewe Alexandra 5 Chesterfield 6, and Chester 12 York City 0. There was only one goalless game in all four divisions – between Aldershot and Bristol City in Third (South). On Boxing Day 1963, a record 66 goals were scored in the ten First Division matches. Top scorers were Fulham who beat Ipswich 10–1, followed by Blackburn, 8–2 winners at West Ham.

BALMY SPELL

Jack Balmer of Liverpool scored only three hat-tricks in his 17-year career. But they came in three consecutive First Division matches in November 1946 – against Portsmouth, Derby County and Arsenal.

MASTER SWITCH

Tried for the first time at centre-forward, Burnley left-winger Louis Page scored a double hat-trick in his team's 7–1 win at Birmingham on 10 April 1926. Rangers' left-winger Davie Wilson also scored six when switched to centre-forward for a game at Falkirk on 17 March 1962. Rangers won 7–1.

BREEN'S BLOOMER

Barnsley's Frank Bokas scored direct from a throw-in

during an FA Cup tie with Manchester United at Oak-well on 22 January 1938. The goal was only allowed to stand because United keeper Tommy Breen made the mistake of touching the ball as it went over his head. The game ended in a 2–2 draw and United won the replay.

MARCO GOALO

Rangers' Marco Negri scored in the first ten Scottish Premier League games of season 1997–8.

GOAL-A-MINUTE SPURS

A goal down at half-time, Spurs scored four times in the space of 4 minutes 44 seconds against Southampton at White Hart Lane on 7 February 1993 to win 4–2.

HEAD BOY

Celtic's Jimmy McGrory scored 50 goals in just 32 League games in 1935–6. Only Partick Thistle and St Johnstone managed to stop him scoring in League games that season. McGrory scored a record 397 League goals for Celtic, nearly half of them with his head. He was so powerful in the air that Queen's Park keeper Jack Harkness once broke three fingers trying to stop a McGrory header. In his entire career for Celtic and

Clydebank, McGrory scored 410 goals in 408 games – the only British footballer to average more than a goal a game.

TON UP

The first man to score 100 goals in both the Scottish and English Leagues was Neil Martin. Having completed his century north of the border with Alloa Athletic, Queen of the South and Hibernian, Martin went on to repeat the feat in England with Sunderland, Coventry City, Nottingham Forest, Brighton and Hove Albion and Crystal Palace. He achieved the double milestone on 21 September 1974 with a goal for Forest against Sheffield Wednesday.

LANDMARK HAT-TRICK

Peter Ndlovu's hat-trick for Coventry City at Liverpool on 1 March 1995 was the first by a visiting player at Anfield since Terry Allcock scored three for Norwich 33 years previously.

HEADS YOU WIN

When Oxford United beat Shrewsbury Town 6–0 in a Second Division match on 23 April 1996, all six goals were headers.

HURST'S HAUL

The last player to score six times in a Football League match was West Ham's Geoff Hurst in the 8–0 thrashing of Sunderland on 19 October 1968.

LIGHTNING START

West Bromwich Albion's Billy Richardson scored four goals in the first five minutes in a First Division game against West Ham on 7 November 1931. Albion ran out the 5–1 winners.

LONG-RANGE HEADER

Aston Villa's Peter Aldis scored with a header from 35 yards against Sunderland in 1952.

98TH TIME LUCKY

After drawing 97 blanks, Danish midfielder John Jensen, scorer of the winning goal in the 1992 European Championships, finally scored for Arsenal in his 98th appearance for the club. The momentous occasion occurred during the game with Queens Park Rangers on the last day of 1994. The shock was clearly too much for his team-mates as Arsenal lost 3–1.

REVENGE IS SWEET

The highest-scoring game in Football League history
was the Third Division (North) encounter between
Tranmere Rovers and Oldham Athletic at Prenton Park
on Boxing Day 1935. Tranmere won 13–4 with Bunny
Bell scoring nine times. Curiously enough when the
two teams had met in the League the previous day at
Oldham, Tranmere had been beaten 4–1.

INSPIRED SUBSTITUTION

Huddersfield Town's Phil Starbuck scored just three
seconds after coming on as a substitute against Wigan
in a Second Division fixture on 12 April 1993.

SECOND-HALF BLITZ

After a goalless first half to their match with Aldershot
in 1935, Exeter City ran amok in the second period and
ended up winning 8–1.

DOUBLE HAT-TRICKS

John Galley managed to score hat-tricks on his debuts
for two clubs. He struck three times on his first
appearance for Rotherham United – at Coventry on
5 December 1964 – and then did the same on his

debut for Bristol City, at Huddersfield on 16 December 1967.

WEMBLEY WIZARDS

Roberto di Matteo's strike after 42 seconds for Chelsea against Middlesbrough in 1997 is the fastest FA Cup Final goal at Wembley. And Bryan Robson's effort after 38 seconds in England's 2–1 win over Yugoslavia in 1989 ranks as the quickest Wembley goal in a first-class match. But the fastest goal in any game at Wembley was the 20–second effort by Maurice Cox for Cambridge University in the 1979 Varsity match.

DEBUT HAT-TRICK

Alan Shearer marked his full First Division debut at the age of 17 by scoring a hat-trick for Southampton in their 4–2 win over Arsenal on 9 April 1988. But Jim Dyet had even greater cause to celebrate after his first appearance for Scottish club King's Park in 1930. For he netted eight times in his side's 12–2 victory over Forfar.

THE SIX THAT GOT AWAY

Denis Law had a field day playing for Manchester City at Luton in an FA Cup fourth round tie on 28 January 1961. He scored six times on a saturated pitch to give City a commanding 6–2 lead, only for conditions to deteriorate to such an extent that the referee was forced to abandon the match after 69 minutes. When the match was replayed, Law could manage only one goal and City crashed out 3–1. Tony Philliskirk had five FA Cup goals disallowed when playing for Peterborough United against Kingstonian in November 1992. With the score at 3–0, the Kingstonian goalkeeper was knocked out by a coin thrown from the crowd and had to leave the field. Peterborough ran out the 9–1 winners but the FA ordered the match to be replayed behind closed doors and this time Peterborough only won 1–0.

SEVEN WAS NOT ENOUGH

St Albans City's Billy Minter scored seven goals against Dulwich Hamlet in an FA Cup fourth qualifying round tie in 1922 . . . and still finished on the losing side. Dulwich won 8–7.

12-GOAL THRILLERS

The highest score draw in Football League history is 6–6 – by Leicester City and Arsenal in Division One on 21 April 1930 and by Charlton Athletic and Middlesbrough in the Second Division on 22 October 1960.

16-GOAL HAUL

Stephan Stanis of Racing Club Lens scored a world

record 16 goals in a wartime French Cup game against Aubry Asturies on 13 December 1942.

LEAST FAVOURITE OPPONENT

Wrexham were glad to see the back of John Jepson in the 1925–6 season after the Accrington Stanley forward had scored three hat-tricks against them in less than five months. His first was in a 5–6 home defeat in Third Division (North) on 24 October, and then on 28 November he struck three times in Accrington's 4–0 win over the Welshmen in the first round of the FA Cup. Finally on 6 March he completed his hat-trick of hat-tricks in the 4–2 League victory at the Racecourse Ground.

RAMPANT RAITH

In season 1937–8, Raith Rovers raced away to the Scottish Second Division title by scoring 142 goals in their 38 League games – an average of over four goals per game.

DEAN'S YEAR

Dixie Dean holds the Football League goalscoring record for a season with the 60 he plundered for Everton in 1927–8. He wound up with nine in the last three games – two against Aston Villa, four at Burnley and three at home to Arsenal. His 60th goal was a trademark header eight minutes from the end of the Arsenal match. Dean also holds the record for the most Football League hat-tricks in a career. He scored 37 for Tranmere and Everton between 1924 and 1938. He died in 1980 at his beloved Goodison Park after collapsing during a "derby" game with Liverpool.

PAYNE'S PLUNDER

Joe Payne scored a Football League record ten goals for Luton against Bristol Rovers in a Third Division (South) fixture on 13 April 1936. Yet amazingly Payne was only a last-minute replacement for Scottish international Billy Boyd and his name was not even in the match-day programme.

4

OI, REF!

A LOCK-IN

Scottish referee David Syme was locked in his dressing-room after a tempestuous 1988 match between Hearts and Rangers . . . by a Hearts director. Douglas Park claimed he locked the door because feelings were running high and because he was worried that the referee might be tackled in his dressing-room. However, a Scottish League committee ruled it "an irresponsible act, particularly as the door was locked for a period of time and no one was aware where the key was. It was in Mr Park's pocket." Park resigned and was fined £1000 by the League.

REFEREE SHOT AT

FIFA banned all international games in Iraq for two years in 1980 after a Malaysian referee had been shot at and robbed following an Olympic qualifying match in Baghdad. Trouble broke out after the referee had awarded a penalty against Iraq, thereby enabling

Kuwait to win 3–2. He was attacked by fans and later two Iraqi football officials burst into his hotel room and fired a revolver at him. Luckily they missed, but the referee subsequently discovered that his wallet containing $500 had gone.

HOT DOG MISSILE

In January 1998, an Oldham fan was ejected from Boundary Park for throwing a hot dog at referee Paul Durkin during a Cup tie with Chelsea.

BACK-BITING

Twenty-three-year-old Italian referee Marcello Donadini was taken to hospital in Bergamo in 1973 after being bitten in the back by a player who didn't agree with a decision.

WALKED OFF

Referee Gary Willard suddenly walked off during a stormy Premiership match between Barnsley and Liverpool at Oakwell in 1998. With both sides looking puzzled, Mr Willard returned five minutes later and restarted the game. Barnsley, who had three players sent off, lost 3–2.

ON THE BLIND SIDE

Swindon striker Iffy Onuora sustained a fractured cheekbone after referee Roger Furnandiz clattered into him during a match with Charlton in 1998.

REF LAID OUT

In November 1970, a clearance from West Ham defender Bobby Moore hit the referee and knocked him out cold. Moore promptly took the ref's whistle and blew it to stop the game.

MIXED EMOTIONS

In 1996, a woman referee who showered with male players was charged by the FA with bringing the game into disrepute. The charge was brought after the Exeter and District Sunday League had received complaints from some of the players' wives. The ref, 41-year-old Janet Fewings, maintained that the lack of facilities forced her to use the same showers as the men.

THANKS, REF

A Barrow shot sailing harmlessly wide struck referee

Ivan Robinson and deflected into the net for the only goal of the 1968 clash with visiting Plymouth.

SAY IT WITH FLOWERS

The Norwegian Football Federation suspended indefinitely international goalkeeper Roy Amundsen in 1981 after he had knocked down and kicked referee Tor Moeien during a Third Division game between Aassiden and Snoegg, a match which Snoegg (Amundsen's team) lost 3–1. The attack left the referee badly concussed and with two broken ribs. Amundsen later visited the ref in hospital and took him some flowers.

CHINESE CHOP

After controversially disallowing a goal and rejecting a penalty appeal in a 1998 Chinese League Cup match between Dalian Wanda and Liaoning Tianrun, top referee Yu Yuancong was promptly sacked by the Chinese FA. The Association explained: "There were serious technical errors that affected the outcome of the match and led to heightened dissatisfaction of competing teams and fans alike."

SURE-FIRE REF

South African referee Lebogang Mokgethi was charged

with murder after allegedly producing a gun and shooting dead a protesting player during a match near Johannesburg in 1998–9. A crowd of 600 saw Wallabies' Isaac Mkhwetha threaten the referee with a knife after the official allowed a goal by the opposition. The referee was then alleged to have whipped out a pistol and shot the player fatally in the chest.

A NAME TO REMEMBER

The 1878 FA Cup Final between Wanderers and Royal Engineers was refereed by a Mr S.R. Bastard.

JIM FIXED IT

In the days before fourth officials, when linesman Denis Drewitt was injured during a First Division game between Arsenal and Liverpool at Highbury in 1972, TV pundit Jimmy Hill – himself a qualified referee – abandoned the ITV commentary-box and took over as linesman for the rest of the match.

REF ABUSED BY LINESMAN

Leicester City midfielder Garry Parker was fined £750 in 1997 for his behaviour while running the line at a Sunday morning match. Parker was charged with misconduct for haranguing the referee while acting as linesman at a Morrells Oxford Sunday League Division Four game between Cherwell Lions and Cowley Cosmos.

RETRIEVED FROM BATH

When Rangers met Nice in a European Champions' Cup tie in 1956, referee Arthur Ellis mistakenly blew for full-time five minutes early. Realising his mistake shortly afterwards, he called the teams back on to the field, including Rangers full-back Eric Caldow who was already in the bath.

NO TURKISH DELIGHT FOR REF

Alpay Ozalan, a defender with Turkish club Besiktas, refused to leave the field after being sent off in a 1998 League match with Gaziantepspor. Instead he started pushing and shoving the referee. Two spectators then ran on to the pitch and one hit the referee on the head before being arrested. Besiktas were fined £2100 and ordered to play their next two home games on neutral grounds.

AN UNEVEN CONTEST

Uruguayan referee Hector Rodriguez marked his first international by sending off the entire Ecuador team in the second half of a 1977 match with . . . Uruguay. First he sent off the Ecuador keeper for time-wasting and then he ordered the rest off one by one as they protested about the dismissal of another of their colleagues for a foul.

"THE BOOK" LOSES THE PLOT

Welsh World Cup referee Clive "The Book" Thomas once added on 45 minutes for stoppages at the end of a game. The match was a boys' club fixture at a pitch on top of a mountain at Blaengwynfi near Thomas's home town of Treorchy. Whenever the ball went out of play, it rolled down the side of the mountain.

SWIFT ACTION

Angered by the abuse which greeted his arrival for the match with Goldenhill Boys Club in 1975, Glasgow referee Mr Tarbet booked all 11 Glencraig United players plus both substitutes in their dressing-room before a ball had even been kicked.

AN UNFAIR COP

A Belgian policeman unwittingly laid out an assistant referee with his truncheon after scuffles broke out at a First Division match in Charleroi in 1998. Charleroi were leading Lierse 2–1 in the 77th minute when referee Jozef Hus sent off a second Lierse player. Fighting broke out among visiting fans and the policeman, in trying to restore order, lashed out with his truncheon and hit referee's assistant Roland Van Nylen. Although Van Nylen quickly recovered and a fourth official was standing by to take over, referee Hus decided to abandon the match. Charleroi were subsequently awarded a 5–0 win.

PLAYERS ATTACKED BY REF

A Bristol Sunday League match between Sea Mills Park and Backwell Sundays in 1998 ended in chaos when two players were attacked by the referee. Kelvin Jenkins – a Sea Mills player serving an eight-match ban for abusing an official – stood in when the assigned referee failed to turn up. But things turned nasty when he punched a striker who called him "whistle happy" and then head-butted a centre-half who tried to intervene. The game was abandoned 15 minutes from the end with Sea Mills leading 3–1 when supporters ran on to the pitch to stop a full-scale fight developing. The Backwell Sundays secretary said afterwards: "His refereeing was actually very good until he started hitting people."

FRIENDLY FIRE

A referee at a friendly game in Brazil in 1968 drew a revolver and shot dead a player who disputed a penalty decision. The ref escaped on horseback.

CHANT BANNED

In 1951, a Dorset referee made an official protest after

the singing of "Oh, Oh! What a Referee!" at a game. As a result the Dorset Football Association formally banned the tune in the county.

DROVE CAR AT REF

Scottish amateur player Robert Crooks was banned for life in 1995 for driving his car on to the pitch at a terrified referee. Crooks was playing for Edinburgh side Telford United against Carrick Hearts when he became incensed by referee Dennis Cunningham's decisions. After running the length of the pitch to abuse the official verbally, Crooks had to be escorted to the changing-rooms. He returned later brandishing a broom handle and was thrown out of the ground, only to return in his car. Luckily the referee managed to dodge the on-coming vehicle.

THE LONG AND THE SHORTS

While refereeing a game between Leeds and Wolves at Elland Road in the 1970s, Tommy Dawes suddenly blew his whistle and summoned Leeds trainer Les Cocker on to the pitch. He then called over Jack Charlton and Norman Hunter of Leeds, along with Wolves' lanky striker Derek Dougan. The group then went into a huddle in the middle of the pitch. The spectators thought Dawes was warning the teams about their tackling but the truth was that the elastic on his shorts had snapped and he had surrounded himself with the three biggest men on the pitch to cover his

embarrassment while he changed into a spare pair
provided by Les Cocker.

LINESMAN FELLED

In January 1998, linesman Edward Martin was knocked
unconscious by a Sheffield United fan after the sending-off of United keeper Simon Tracey during the First
Division game at Portsmouth.

REFEREE STONED (1)

There is nothing new about fans showing their dis-
pleasure at referees. As long ago as 1902, angry Sunderland fans stoned the referee's carriage as it left Roker
Park following the Wearsiders' 1–0 defeat to Sheffield
Wednesday.

REFEREE STONED (2)

A Tanzanian soccer match was postponed in January
1978 after the referee was arrested on the pitch and
accused of smoking marijuana just before the kick-off!

AIR-LIFTED TO SAFETY

A referee and his linesmen had to be rescued by

helicopter from 5000 bottle-throwing Italian fans after Palermo lost 3–2 at home to Napoli in 1969. The police helicopter landed on the pitch and scooped the officials to safety as the crowd pelted them with missiles.

5

UP FOR THE CUP

FAIR PLAY

On 3 January 1997, Leicester City went through their entire third round tie with Northampton at Filbert Street without committing a single foul. Leicester won 4–0.

FOGGED OFF

Colchester United's record crowd of 19,072 turned out to watch a first round FA Cup tie with Reading in 1948, only for the game to be abandoned after 35 minutes because of fog.

PIZZA PARADE

Not surprisingly, Bolton's 2–0 victory over post-Munich Manchester United in the 1958 Cup Final wasn't particularly well received in Manchester. So as the Cup-winners' coach passed through Manchester en route to Bolton, the Bolton players were pelted with tomatoes and flour.

WELSH WINNERS

The only non-English team to win the FA Cup are Cardiff City. They beat Arsenal 1–0 in 1927, the winning goal being a shot from Hugh Ferguson which slid through the arms of Arsenal's Welsh international keeper Dan Lewis. The Arsenal hierarchy blamed Lewis's gaffe on the fact that he was wearing a new jersey, the sheen of which had stopped him holding on to the ball. From then on, Arsenal made sure that every new goalkeeper's jersey was softened up in the wash before being worn on the field of play.

THE MAGNIFICENT NINE

Nine players have scored in every round of the FA Cup in the same season – Sandy Brown of Tottenham Hotspur in 1901, Ellis Rimmer of Sheffield Wednesday in 1935, Frank O'Donnell of Preston North End in 1937, Stan Mortensen of Blackpool in 1948, Jackie Milburn of Newcastle United in 1951, Nat Lofthouse of Bolton Wanderers in 1953, Charlie Wayman of Preston North End in 1954, Jeff Astle of West Bromwich Albion in 1968, and Peter Osgood of Chelsea in 1970.

SCOUSE RIVALS

Liverpool and Everton have met each other more than any other two clubs in the history of the FA Cup. They have met 20 times with Liverpool winning nine and Everton six. The second most popular meeting is Everton versus Sheffield Wednesday. Those two have faced each other in the Cup on 19 occasions.

QUEEN'S MISS OUT

Queen's Park are the only Scottish side to reach the FA Cup Final. They did so in 1884 and 1885, but lost on both occasions to Blackburn Rovers.

TOO-PROUD PRESTON

All-conquering Preston North End were so confident of beating West Bromwich Albion in the 1888 FA Cup Final that they asked to be photographed with the trophy before the game, pointing out that they were likely to be dirty afterwards. Hearing this, the match referee asked: "Had you not better win it first?" Wise words, for Preston slumped to a shock 2–1 defeat.

INDIAN SIGN

Bob Stokoe was something of a jinx figure for Don

Revie, having twice beaten him in FA Cup Finals. In 1955 Stokoe, a centre-half for Newcastle United, marked Manchester City centre-forward Revie out of the game, enabling United to win 3–1. And then in 1973, Stokoe managed unfancied Second Division Sunderland to their epic Wembley triumph against Revie's mighty Leeds.

MUCH-TRAVELLED

Nottingham Forest are the only Football League club to have played FA Cup ties in all four home countries. In 1885 they travelled to Edinburgh for a semi-final replay against Queen's Park; they played at Linfield in the first round of the 1889 competition; and in 1922 they were beaten in the third round at Cardiff City.

A DAY TO FORGET

Among the Leicester City team humbled 1–0 by Isthmian Leaguers Harlow Town in the third round of the FA Cup on 8 January 1980 was a young Gary Lineker.

UNITED SHAKEN

The last time Manchester United were drawn against a non-League team in the FA Cup was back in 1953 when

Walthamstow Avenue shook the soccer world by drawing 1–1 at Old Trafford. But the dream ended there as United won the replay at Highbury 5–2.

LONGEST TIE

The longest FA Cup tie was a fourth qualifying round contest between Alvechurch and Oxford City in 1971–2. It took six matches and 11 hours before Alvechurch finally won through to the first round proper . . . where they promptly lost 4–2 at Aldershot.

ONE-EYED FINALIST

Bob Thomson was the only one-eyed player ever to appear in an FA Cup Final. He was a member of the Chelsea team which lost 3–0 to Sheffield United in 1915.

21 UNBEATEN

Between May 1978, when they lost in the final to Ipswich, and May 1980, when they were beaten at Wembley by West Ham, Arsenal went 21 FA Cup matches unbeaten. This included a number of replays, notably the five matches it took to get past Sheffield Wednesday in the third round in 1979.

SIMPLY THE BEST

On 7 February 1970, in his first game back after serving a four-week suspension, George Best scored six of Manchester United's goals at Northampton in the fifth round of the FA Cup. United strolled to an 8–2 victory.

CARTER THE UNSTOPPABLE GOAL MACHINE

Raich Carter was the only player to be a member of FA Cup winning teams before and after the Second World War. In 1937 he helped Sunderland defeat Preston 3–1 and in 1946 he inspired Derby to a 4–1 victory over Charlton. It wasn't such a happy story for Willie Fagan. Part of the beaten Preston team in 1937, he tasted a second Cup Final defeat in 1950 as Liverpool went down 2–0 to Arsenal.

CUP CHUMPS

Of current clubs who joined the Football League before the Second World War, only Hartlepool United and Torquay United have never reached the last 16 of the FA Cup.

BRAVE BERT

Manchester City goalkeeper Bert Trautmann played the last 15 minutes of the 1956 FA Cup Final against Birmingham City with a broken neck. The damage was done when the German-born keeper dived at the feet of Birmingham's Peter Murphy. Trautmann continued playing in extreme pain, being forced to hold on to the goalposts just to stay on his feet, although the full extent of his injury was not revealed until a post-match X-ray. His heroics helped his team to a 3–1 triumph.

THE TWO DEGREES

The Liverpool Cup Final sides of 1971 and 1974 boasted two university graduates – Steve Heighway and Brian Hall.

DOUBLE DOSE OF DESPONDENCY

Four clubs have reached the FA Cup Final in the same season that they were relegated – Manchester City (1926), Leicester City (1969), Brighton & Hove Albion (1983) and Middlesbrough (1997). And all four lost at Wembley. In 1915 Chelsea lost in the Cup Final as well as finishing second from bottom of the First Division. But the First World War saved them from relegation and when League football resumed in 1919, Division One was extended, enabling Chelsea to retain their place in the top flight.

THE ULTIMATE REVENGE

On 12 December 1953, non-League Cambridge United were knocked out of the FA Cup at the second round stage 2–1 by Bradford Park Avenue from Third Division (North). Cambridge exacted the ultimate revenge 17 years later when they were voted into the Football League at the expense of Bradford.

A NEAR THING

Worksop Town of the Midland League came within inches of springing the biggest FA Cup upset of all time. In the first round of the 1922–3 competition, they were drawn at home to First Division Tottenham Hotspur. Deciding to surrender home advantage and play at White Hart Lane, Worksop held Spurs to a goalless draw. And it could have been so much worse for the League aristocrats as little Worksop hit the bar with just four minutes remaining. But Spurs made no mistakes the second time and romped to a 9–0 win.

TOP SCORERS

Henry Cursham of Notts County holds the record for most FA Cup goals in a career with 48 between 1880 and 1887. His closest rival was Ian Rush (Chester City, Liverpool and Newcastle United) who scored 44 between 1979 and 1998.

PLAY IT AGAIN, ARSENE

Arsenal offered to replay their Cup tie against Sheffield United in 1999 after breaking the unwritten rule about returning the ball to the opposition following an injury. Marc Overmars' controversial goal from Kanu's centre had given the Gunners a 2–1 victory but the result left a bad taste in both camps. So the FA agreed to a replay which Arsenal duly won fair and square.

FANTASY ISLAND

The last time that a club from off the mainland knocked a League team out of the FA Cup was in 1945 when Newport (Isle of Wight) beat Clapton Orient 3–2 over the two legs of their first round tie. The plucky islanders crashed out 12–0 on aggregate to Aldershot in the next round.

FAWLTY BEHAVIOUR

Glasgow Rangers' sole foray in the FA Cup was in 1886–7 when they were drawn away to Everton in the first round. Before the match, the Scots planned to stay overnight in a Liverpool hotel but the proprietor threw the players and their luggage out on to the street in the early hours of the morning because they were too rowdy. They managed to find another hotel and overcame their lack of sleep to win the tie 1–0. Rangers' Cup run ended in a 3–1 semi-final defeat to Aston Villa. Before that match, they were entertained to a meal by former colleague Hugh McIntyre. But goalkeeper Willie Chalmers overdid the hospitality and his lack of mobility was responsible for all three Villa goals.

CLOUGH HUMBLED

Barnsley manager Dave Bassett was a member of the Walton & Hersham team which inflicted Brian Clough's greatest managerial humiliation. During Clough's ill-fated reign at Brighton, the south coast side were drawn away to Isthmian Leaguers Walton in the first round of the FA Cup in November 1973. The game ended in a 0–0 draw but in the replay at the Goldstone Ground, Walton ran out the sensational 4–0 winners. Fourteen months later, Bassett was in the Wimbledon side which won 1–0 at Burnley, making the Dons the first non-League team to win away to a First Division side in the Cup since Darlington beat Sheffield Wednesday back in 1920.

HOBBLING BOBBY

West Ham's Bobby Gould was taken off at half-time in a third round FA Cup tie at Southampton on 6 January 1975 when it was discovered that he had been playing for the past half-hour with a broken leg. In that time he had even managed to head a goal to help the Hammers towards a 2–1 victory.

WE'LL MEET AGAIN

The only clubs to have met each other in three FA Cup

Finals are Aston Villa and West Bromwich Albion (1887, 1892 and 1895) and Arsenal and Newcastle (1932, 1952 and 1998).

WASHED UP AT BOURNEMOUTH

Manchester United travelled to Bournemouth for a third round FA Cup tie on 7 January 1984 with only one away defeat in the League all season. By contrast, Bournemouth were fourth from bottom of Division Three with just five home wins to their name. The previous Monday, United had drawn at Anfield while Bournemouth lost at bottom-of-the-table Port Vale. Yet on the day, Bournemouth overcame United 2–0. Shortly afterwards, United beat Barcelona in the European Cup Winners' Cup. Manager Ron Atkinson recalled: "I told Maradona he could think himself lucky he hadn't been playing Bournemouth!"

ANOTHER FINE MESS

Bradford Park Avenue's record FA Cup victory was an 11–0 thrashing of Denby Dale in a second qualifying round tie in 1908. Yet it was achieved by Bradford's reserves since on the same day the first team were playing a League match which clearly took priority. In view of the Cup score, it was somewhat ironic that the FA fined Park Avenue £50 for not fielding their strongest side.

LATE DRAMA

Chelsea won an FA Cup fourth round second replay at home to Preston on 3 February 1969 despite going a goal down in the 90th minute. David Webb and Charlie Cooke scored in the two minutes of injury time to give Chelsea a dramatic 2–1 success. It was no more than Chelsea deserved really because, having drawn 0–0 up at Deepdale, they were leading the first replay 2–0 when the floodlights failed in the 72nd minute. So the tie went to a third game.

LUCKY HORSESHOE

As Sheffield Wednesday winger Ellis Rimmer trooped off at half-time in the 1935 FA Cup Final against West Bromwich Albion, a woman supporter thrust a horseshoe into his hand for good luck. It proved a good omen as Rimmer scored twice in the last five minutes to give Wednesday a 4–2 victory.

OPPOSITE NUMBERS

When Colchester United knocked Bradford Park Avenue out of the FA Cup in 1948, the Colchester centre-half was Ted Fenton and his opposite number was Ron Greenwood. Thirteen years later Fenton was succeeded by Greenwood as manager of West Ham.

OLD BOYS WREAK HAVOC

The Boston United side which humbled Derby County 6–1 at the Baseball Ground in a second round FA Cup tie on 10 December 1955 contained no fewer than six former Derby players. The two teams met again in the Cup in 1974. This time it was Derby's turn to win 6–1.

FOREST FEAT

Only one of the current League clubs got as far as the semi-final of the FA Cup at the first attempt – Nottingham Forest in 1879. What's more, they repeated the feat a year later.

MYSTERY SOLVED

The original FA Cup was stolen from a Birmingham shop window in 1895. It was never recovered and its fate remained a mystery for a further 63 years until an 80-year-old local man finally confessed. He said that he and two accomplices, both of whom were now dead, had taken the Cup and that it had been melted down to make counterfeit half-crowns, some of which were passed on at a nearby pub.

FOUR-TIME LOSER

Paul Bracewell picked up three FA Cup losers' medals in

six years . . . all against Liverpool. In 1986 and 1989 he was a member of the defeated Everton teams and in 1992 he was in the Sunderland side beaten 2–0. Just to underline that Wembley wasn't his happiest hunting ground, in 1985 he had been part of the Everton team beaten by Manchester United in the final.

DIXIE'S CUP

Wrexham's Dixie McNeill scored in ten successive FA Cup rounds between 1977 and 1980.

LESSON LEARNED

A year after being routed 13–2 by Spurs in the FA Cup, Fourth Division Crewe Alexandra returned to London to take on Chelsea – Jimmy Greaves, Terry Venables and all – in a third round tie on 7 January 1961. It was a happier journey home for the 6000 Crewe fans this time as their side pulled off a shock 2–1 win.

FIRST TOUCH

On 10 January 1989, Watford scored with their first touch of the ball in an FA Cup third round replay with visiting Newcastle. United keeper Dave Beasant was penalised for handling the ball outside the area and Watford's Neil Redfearn scored from the resultant free-kick. The match ended in a 2–2 draw, Newcastle eventually progressing after a third replay.

NORTHERN SUPREMACY

After Old Etonians lifted the FA Cup in 1882, it was a further 19 years before another southern team captured the trophy. Spurs beat Sheffield United in 1901.

MEDAL MUDDLE

At the medal presentation after the 1992 FA Cup Final, Sunderland, who had just lost 2–0 to Liverpool, were mistakenly handed the winners' medals

WOLVES REV UP

Among Wolves' scorers when they beat Newcastle 3–1 in the 1908 FA Cup Final was a vicar! The Rev. Kenneth Hunt scored their first goal against the Magpies and so became the only clergyman to collect an FA Cup winners' medal. Rumour has it that when he told his teammates that God was on their side, the referee demanded to know why his name wasn't on the team-sheet . . .

COSTLY OVERSIGHT

Birmingham City were unable to take part in the FA Cup in 1921 because they forgot to post the entry form.

EIGHT-YEAR DROUGHT

After defeating Mansfield Town 3–0 in the third round in 1960, Blackpool went another eight years without winning an FA Cup tie. They finally ended their losing streak with a 2–1 win against Chesterfield in a third round tie on 27 January 1968.

PITCH INVASION FLOORS FOREST

After 55 minutes of their sixth round FA Cup tie at St James' Park on 9 March 1974, Nottingham Forest led Newcastle United 3–1. To make matters worse for the Geordies, defender Pat Howard had just been sent off. The crowd didn't like it one bit and 500 of them invaded the pitch. Two Forest players were attacked and referee Gordon Kew was forced to take the players off. Eventually the police restored order and the teams returned, but by now Forest were shell-shocked. They conceded three late goals to go down 4–3. But Newcastle celebrations were cut short when the FA ordered the match to be replayed on a neutral ground because Forest had been intimidated by the crowd. After a goalless draw, Newcastle scraped through in a third match 1–0 and went on to Wembley where they met their match in Liverpool.

THE LONG AND WINDING ROAD

The road to winning the FA Cup was a long one for Barnsley in 1912. They played a record 12 matches, including six replays, one of them in the final itself.

FINALIST FOR THREE CLUBS

In the space of seven years, Ernie Taylor played for three different clubs in the FA Cup Final. In 1951 he appeared for Newcastle United, in 1953 he played for Blackpool and in 1958 for Manchester United.

BUCHAN'S BOAST

Martin Buchan has the distinction of being the only player to captain both English and Scottish FA Cup winning sides. He skippered Aberdeen in 1970 and Manchester United in 1977.

THE MAGIC LAMP

Huddersfield Town were convinced that an Aladdin's Lamp, presented to them by a pantomime director, was bringing them luck in the 1919–20 season. All of the players made a point of rubbing their boots on the lucky lamp before leaving the dressing-room and, sure enough, they won promotion to the First Division. They also reached the FA Cup Final at Stamford Bridge, but there the lamp's magic wore off at last. For Huddersfield lost 1–0 to Aston Villa, the only goal of the game being diverted into the net off the neck of Huddersfield centre-half Tom Wilson.

MARK FOUR

The only player to pick up four FA Cup winners' medals

in the twentieth century was Mark Hughes – three with Manchester United (1985, 1990 and 1994) and one with Chelsea (1997). He only tasted defeat in the final in 1995 when United lost to Everton.

MISGUIDED PROTEST

Kidderminster Harriers launched a protest after losing 3–1 at Darwen in the first round of the FA Cup on 17 January 1891. The FA upheld the complaint and ordered the tie to be replayed. This time Darwen won 13–0.

HANDY ANDY

Andy Locke scored a hat-trick in two minutes 20 seconds for Nantwich against Droylesden in an FA Cup first qualifying round tie on 9 September 1995.

THE CROWD WAS UNSIGHTED

A crowd of 42,000 – at the time a record for a game in London – turned up at Crystal Palace to see Aston Villa play West Bromwich Albion in the 1895 FA Cup Final. But because of mass confusion at the turnstiles, most of the crowd missed the only goal of the game, scored by Villa's Bob Chatt after just 30 seconds.

POTTERS' WAIL

Stoke City are the only founder members of the Football League still in existence not to have won the FA Cup.

LOANEE LES

Les Sealey became the first "on loan" player to appear in an FA Cup Final when he kept goal for Manchester United in the 1990 replay at Crystal Palace. Sealey was on loan from Luton at the time and had only played two League games for United prior to the final. Jim Leighton played in the first match but Sealey stepped in for the replay and kept a clean sheet.

I'M FREE

Not one member of Bolton Wanderers' FA Cup winning team of 1958 cost the club a transfer fee.

NON-LEAGUE WINNERS

Spurs are the only team to have won the FA Cup as a non-League side. When they lifted the trophy in 1901, they were members of the Southern League. No team from outside the top two divisions has ever reached the Cup Final although Chesterfield were desperately unlucky not to do so in 1997. The last club from outside the top flight to win the Cup were West Ham in 1980.

BOGEY TEAM

In four FA Cup meetings between the two teams, the most recent in 1995, Chelsea have lost to Millwall every time.

CAPLESS WONDERS

Sunderland, in 1973, were the last team to win the FA Cup without an international in their line-up.

UNSUNG HERO

Mike Trebilcock played only 11 League games in three seasons for Everton. But in that time the unknown Cornishman scored twice in the 1966 FA Cup Final to guide Everton to a 3–2 win over Sheffield Wednesday.

LUCKY SPURS

Spurs have won on eight of their nine appearances in

the FA Cup Final. The exception was in 1987 when they lost to Coventry City. Conversely, Leicester City have appeared in four FA Cup Finals and lost the lot.

CUP SPECIALIST

Although Arthur Turner won an FA Cup winner's medal with Charlton Athletic in 1946, he never actually played a League game for the club. There was no League football in the 1945–6 season and he had left The Valley before the start of the following campaign.

A PAIR OF CHARLIES

When Sunderland met Aston Villa in the 1913 FA Cup Final, they had a player called Charles Thomson in their line-up. And the next time they reached the final in 1937, against Preston, they had another Charles Thomson in their side.

DISMAL DALE

Between the two World Wars, Rochdale won just ties in the FA Cup proper – and neither of those was against League opposition. In 1925, they defeated North Eastern Leaguers West Stanley 4–0 and two years later they hammered Crook Town 8–2. Then that was it until after

Hitler's downfall, the miserable run finally coming to an end with a 2–1 triumph at Stockport on 17 November 1945.

DERBY HUDDLE

Following a goalless first half to their second round FA Cup tie at Lincoln on 8 February 1902, Derby County kicked off the second half in a huddle. Eight of their players surrounded the ball, preventing any Lincoln player from getting to it. The Derby circle shepherded the ball into the Lincoln penalty area where Ben Warren scored what turned out to be the first of a hat-trick in Derby's 3–1 win.

DONS' DOUBLE

Wimbledon are the only club to have won the FA Cup and the FA Amateur Cup.

ANGLO-FREE

The Liverpool FA Cup-winning team of 1986 didn't contain a solitary English player. Mark Lawrenson was born in Preston but played for the Republic of Ireland. The rest were made up of four Scots, two Irishmen, a Welshman, a Dane, an Australian and a Zimbabwean. The last team to win the Cup with 11 Englishmen was West Ham back in 1975.

NEAR MISSES

Seven clubs have finished as runners-up in the League and FA Cup in the same season – Huddersfield Town (1927–8), Arsenal (1931–2), Wolverhampton Wanderers (1938–9), Burnley (1961–2), Leeds United (1964–5 and 1969–70), Everton (1985–6) and Manchester United (1994–5).

KINNAIRD'S MONOPOLY

The Hon. Arthur Kinnaird played in no fewer than nine of the first 12 FA Cup Finals. He was victorious five times – with The Wanderers in 1873, 1877 and 1878, and with Old Etonians in 1879 and 1882. On the downside, he also had the unwanted honour of being the first player to score an own goal in a Cup Final when he put the ball into his own net when playing for The Wanderers against Oxford University in 1877.

NEIGHBOURING ATTRACTIONS

On 22 November 1952, three FA Cup ties were staged within a stone's throw of each other in East London. Leyton Orient entertained Bristol Rovers, Isthmian Leaguers Leytonstone were at home to Watford, and Leyton from the Athenian League were playing host to Hereford United. None of the three neighbours won.

GETTING SHIRTY

At the end of the 1970 FA Cup Final, Chelsea's David Webb was refused his winners' medal because he was wearing a Leeds shirt. He had swapped shirts with one of the Leeds players after the game, as a result of which an FA official became convinced that Webb was a Leeds player.

SECOND THOUGHTS

Whenever West Ham have appeared in an FA Cup Final, a Second Division team has been involved. In 1923 and 1980 the Hammers themselves were in Division Two while in 1964 and 1975 they beat Second Division opponents in the shape of Preston and Fulham respectively.

LUCKY NUMBER

Spurs have a knack of winning the FA Cup when the year ends in a "1". They have won it in 1901, 1921, 1961, 1981 and 1991.

SOUTHEND HAVE NO PEERS

Southend United scored a total of 19 goals in the first two rounds of the 1968–9 FA Cup. They beat King's Lynn 9–0 in round one and then trounced Brentwood 10–1 in round two.

BARREN RUN

Leeds United went 16 matches without a win in the FA Cup between 1952 and 1963. This miserable run included three successive years when they lost 2–1 at home to Cardiff in the third round.

THE LUCK OF THE DRAW

When Manchester United won the FA Cup in 1990, they played every game away from home. But the victorious 1999 United team benefited from a home draw in every round. Back in 1948, United became the only club to win the Cup despite meeting top-division opponents in every round. They disposed of Aston Villa, Liverpool, Charlton Athletic, Preston North End, Derby County and, finally, Blackpool.

SAM'S REMEDY

Charlton goalkeeper Sam Bartram played against Newcastle in the 1947 FA Cup semi-final with a hot poultice on his stomach to counter food poisoning. Despite the restriction to his movement, Bartram and Charlton won 4–0.

6

SICK AS A PARROT

MONKEY BUSINESS

Desperate to attend a Rumbelows Cup replay with
Peterborough in 1992, a teenage Middlesbrough fan
thought he had got round a court curfew by disguis-
ing himself in a gorilla suit. But when Boro scored
the only goal of the game, he threw the head into
the air in celebration and was subsequently spotted
by a police officer watching the highlights on TV at
home.

SECOND-CLASS POST

Bournemouth forward Reg Cutler broke a goalpost after
running into it during a 1957 Cup tie with Wolves at
Molineux. There was a seven-minute delay while the
post was repaired. Remarkably, Cutler recovered to
score the only goal of the game.

THE MISSING KEEPER

Brighton goalkeeper Perry Digweed had a good excuse for not turning up for a game with Bournemouth in September 1988 – nobody at the club had actually told him that he was supposed to be playing.

HOUNDED OUT

Brentford goalkeeper Chic Brodie was literally hounded out of the game. Playing against Colchester in 1970, he was patrolling his goalmouth when a mongrel dog ran on to the pitch and crashed into him with such force that Brodie severely damaged the ligaments in his knee. The injury effectively ended his career.

GERMAN INEFFICIENCY

The kick-off for the 1974 World Cup Final in Munich was delayed when it was realised that there were no corner flags on the pitch.

WASTED JOURNEY

England cricketer Mickey Stewart was desperate to appear in the 1956 FA Amateur Cup Final for Corinthian Casuals even though he was touring with the willow in West Indies at the time. Undeterred by the distance, he abandoned the Caribbean tour and set off on the 4500-mile journey from the West Indies to Wembley. It took him two and a half days, but, alas, he arrived at the Twin Towers three minutes after kick-off and so could only watch the game from the bench. To make matters worse, Casuals crashed 4–1 to Bishop Auckland.

NO KRUSE CONTROL

Torquay United defender Pat Kruse holds the unwanted record of scoring the quickest own goal in the Football League. Kruse's aberration came against Cambridge United in a Fourth Division game on 8 January 1977 when he headed past his own keeper after just eight seconds. The fastest own goal in the top flight came courtesy of Arsenal's Steve Bould at Sheffield Wednesday on 17 February 1990. He put the ball into his own net after 16 seconds.

SNOW JOKE

Gillingham skipper Mark Weatherley trudged six miles through deep snow drifts to join his team for a 1987 FA Cup tie with Wigan. When he arrived at the ground, he found that the match was off.

GREY DAY

After being given the runaround by Southampton in April 1996, Manchester United swapped shirts at half-time. The United players complained that their grey away kit, which they had worn in the first half, made it difficult for them to pick each other out against the crowd. So they changed to a blue strip for the second period but, 3–0 down already, were unable to save the game.

SPARSE CROWD

Only 450 people turned up to watch Rochdale entertain Cambridge United in a Third Division fixture on 2 February 1974 – the lowest Football League attendance since the war.

FOSTER'S FLOP

Brighton & Hove Albion captain Steve Foster was so distraught at the prospect of missing his side's 1983 FA Cup Final with Manchester United through suspension that he took his case to the High Court. He lost and could only sit on the sidelines as Brighton held United to a 2–2 draw. But the good news was he was back for the replay. This time, with Foster in the side, Brighton lost 4–0.

A DAY TO FORGET

Playing for Stockport County against Fulham in 1913, Norman Wood headed an own goal, gave away a penalty for handball from which Fulham scored, and then missed a penalty himself. Stockport lost 3–1.

TAKING THE MAIK

Goalkeeper Maik Taylor is unlikely to forget his League debut in a hurry. Playing for Barnet against Hereford in August 1995, Taylor could only look on helplessly as a wind-assisted kick from his opposite number Chris Mackenzie sailed over his head and into the net.

BLOW-OUT FOR DUNLOP

Lightning struck twice in the case of Linfield goalkeeper George Dunlop. In August 1988 he was beaten by a huge clearance from debut-making Cliftonville keeper Andy McLean. Then eight months later, in the 1989 Roadferry Cup Final, Dunlop was again left with egg on his face as a massive punt from Glentoran keeper Alan Paterson ended up in the Linfield net.

THREE-TIME LOSERS

Middlesbrough reached three Wembley finals in two years . . . and lost the lot. In 1997, they lost to Leicester City in the Coca-Cola Cup (in a replay at Hillsborough) and to Chelsea in the FA Cup. Then in 1998 they were beaten by Chelsea in the Coca-Cola Cup.

CARELESS HANDS

Voted Leicester City's 1995–6 Player of the Year for his safe hands, goalkeeper Kevin Poole was presented with a cut-glass rose bowl . . . which he promptly dropped.

RIGHT TIME, WRONG PLAICE

Following a pre-match meal of plaice, four Stoke players were taken ill during the first half of the Division One game at Liverpool in 1902. The first to leave the field with stomach cramps was goalkeeper Dick Roose after just ten minutes and three more stayed in the dressing-room at half-time. Stoke started the second half with seven men although two of the infirm did eventually manage to stagger back on to the pitch. But goalkeeper Roose was not among them. Stoke lost 7–0.

PHANTOM WHISTLER

Arsenal full-back Dennis Evans scored just about the most bizarre own goal ever seen at Highbury, against Blackpool in 1955. With Arsenal leading 4–0 and only moments to go, a spectator in the crowd blew a whistle. The Arsenal players thought it was the referee's final whistle and Evans booted the ball towards his own goal. It sailed past keeper Sullivan who was bending down to retrieve his cap from the back of the net. It was only then that it dawned on them that the whistle they had heard was not the referee's and that the match was still in progress.

HIS NAME WAS MUD

In March 1991, controversial Rangers striker Mo Johnston missed a sitter against Aberdeen. He was so annoyed with himself that he picked up a piece of mud and hurled it to the ground. In doing so, he cricked his back, ruling himself out of the next match.

HARDWICK'S HOWLER

George Hardwick, who later went on to captain England, put through his own goal within a minute of his debut for Middlesbrough against Bolton on 18 December 1937.

A NEATE SOLUTION

Shortly before the start of the 1986–7 season, Reading groundsman Gordon Neate accidentally sprayed the Elm Park pitch with concentrated weedkiller instead of a selective solution. His blunder ruined 75 per cent of the playing surface and forced the club to cancel its pre-season friendlies.

CHEEKY CROSBY

Manchester City goalkeeper Andy Dibble was left red-faced during a 1990 clash with Nottingham Forest at the City Ground. Having collected the ball safely, Dibble balanced it on the palm of his hand in readiness to clear upfield. But Forest winger Gary Crosby crept up behind him, headed the ball off his hand and turned it into the net. To Dibble's astonishment, the goal was allowed to stand.

UNLUCKY 13

Halifax Town reserve goalkeeper Steve Milton made a nightmare start to his League career. Called up to face

Stockport County in a Division Three (North) match on
6 January 1934, the hapless Milton let in 13 goals, 11 of
them in the second half.

HIGH JINX

After scoring the winner for Arsenal against Sheffield
Wednesday in the 1993 Coca-Cola Cup Final – his first
goal for the club – Steve Morrow ended up with a
broken arm. The culprit was his own captain, Tony
Adams, who, in celebration at the end of the game,
hoisted Morrow on to his shoulders and then dropped
him.

UNLUCKY BREAKS

After breaking his arm in a match at Leicester in
1998–9, Southampton defender Francis Benali did it
again a month later while sweeping up leaves in his
garden.

DOUBLE TROUBLE

In the space of four days in 1972, Everton defender
Tommy Wright twice contrived to score own goals
inside the first minute. On 4 March he put through
his own goal in the Merseyside derby with Liverpool at
Anfield and then repeated the feat against Manchester
United at Old Trafford.

NO HAPPY RETURNS

Due to an injury crisis at the club, Bournemouth coach Harry Redknapp was forced to come out of retirement and play his first senior game for four and a half years in the Milk Cup tie with Manchester United at Old Trafford on 6 October 1982. There was no happy return for Redknapp as he put through his own goal after 28 minutes to help United to a 2–0 win.

SALAD DAYS

Chelsea keeper Dave Beasant was ruled out of action for the start of the 1993–4 season after dropping a jar of salad cream on his big toe. Beasant had tried to catch the falling jar with his right foot but ended up severing the tendon.

BEES STUNG

Playing at Bristol Rovers in 1996, Brentford keeper Kevin Dearden was confused by a whistle in the crowd. Thinking the referee had blown for offside, Dearden put the ball down for a free-kick and watched Rovers' Marcus Browning knock the ball into the empty net. Rovers won 2–1. Rotherham keeper Jim McDonagh made a similar blunder against Bolton in 1972. Thinking that the ball had gone out of play, he put it down for a goal-kick but Bolton's Garry Jones played on and nipped in to score.

ALLO, ALLO, ALLO

Nottinghamshire policemen who played against the Lincolnshire force at Scunthorpe in 1959 returned to their dressing-room after the match to find that someone had been through their pockets and stolen a quantity of cash.

WE WUZ ROBBED!

Hard-up Cardiff City were delighted when their third round FA Cup tie with visiting Queens Park Rangers in 1990 brought record gate receipts of £50,000. But they weren't as thrilled on the Monday morning when they went to the safe and discovered that the money had been stolen over the weekend.

GOTTA PICK A POCKET OR TWO

Back in the 1950s, there was considerable opposition to the staging of evening floodlit matches because it was feared they would encourage crime. These fears proved well founded at an evening Cup tie between Everton and Sunderland in 1958 when pickpockets stole £159 10s from spectators.

SPELL CHECK NEEDED

After losing all 14 games at the start of the 1993 season, Thetford Town players were hypnotised in an attempt to improve their fortunes. They lost their next game 9–0.

CHANNEL HOPPING

Liverpool striker Robbie Fowler was sidelined with a knee injury sustained by stretching to pick up the remote control for the TV.

BACK TO THE DRAWING BOARD

City authorities in Verona who planned to name a new stadium in memory of Italy's 1938 World Cup winning goalkeeper Aldo Olivieri scrapped the idea in 1996 after discovering that he was still alive.

OTHERWISE ENGAGED

Spurs forwards Les Ferdinand and Ruel Fox missed the start of the second half of the club's game at Newcastle in October 1997 after accidentally getting themselves locked in the toilet.

7

STADIUM ANNOUNCEMENTS

BLACK NIGHT

Derby County's first game at their new Pride Park stadium – on 13 August 1997 – ended in chaos after 55 minutes when the floodlights failed. The match with Wimbledon was abandoned with Derby leading 2–1.

MAINE MEN

Manchester United didn't install floodlights at Old Trafford until 1957 and so had to play their early European Cup ties at Maine Road.

CARTED OFF

When Arsenal played their first game at Highbury, against Leicester Fosse in 1913, the ground was still being completed. The facilities were so poor that a player who was injured in the game had to be carried away on a milk cart!

EVERTON AT ANFIELD

Everton, not Liverpool, were the original tenants of Anfield. They played there between 1884 and 1892 until they fell out with their landlord, the local MP, over a rent increase. It was only then that Liverpool FC was formed.

WATKIN'S FOLLY

Wembley Stadium was only built in the first place because a man called Edward Watkin wanted to erect a rival monument to the Eiffel Tower. In 1901 workmen started constructing Watkin's 1150-foot-high tower on a site at Wembley. But it reached a height of only 200 feet before the concrete foundations collapsed and the project was abandoned. Watkin's Folly, as it became known, dominated the north-west London skyline for another 20 years until the government decided to pull it down and build a magnificent new stadium to house the 1924 British Empire Exhibition.

SAFETY FIRST

Before Wembley Stadium staged the first FA Cup Final

in 1923, an infantry battalion and hundreds of local volunteers spent 15 minutes marching up and down the terraces to test their strength and safety.

OLDEST RESIDENTS

Chesterfield have been at their ground longer than any other Football League Club. They have played at Saltergate since their formation in 1866, beating Preston North End (Deepdale since 1881), Burnley (Turf Moor since 1882) and Darlington (Feethams since 1883). Incidentally Preston's first match at Deepdale was hardly auspicious – they lost 16–0 to Blackburn Rovers in a friendly.

PAL JOEY

When Watford used to play at their Cassio Road ground, the local character was a guy named Joey Goodchild who used to climb on to the roof of the stand and do a tap dance for the crowd. But one day he fell off and landed on a lady spectator, and the club had to pay her £25 by way of compensation.

HIGHS AND LOWS

The highest Football League ground above sea level is West Bromwich Albion's The Hawthorns at 541 feet. The lowest is Norwich City's Carrow Road at 6 feet 6 inches.

JOINED-UP WRITING

Faced with an unprecedented demand from journalists to cover the club's fourth round FA Cup tie with First Division Sunderland on 29 January 1949, Yeovil Town were forced to import a quantity of desks from a nearby junior school. The scribes had plenty to write about as Yeovil recorded an epic 2–1 triumph.

IN THE DARK

The last Football League club to install floodlights was Chesterfield, in 1967. The last Scottish League club to have lights was Stranraer, in 1981.

SHORT STAY

Clapton Orient played two Third Division (South) matches at Wembley Stadium in the 1930–1 season while their own ground was out of use. But when only 2500 fans turned up to their second game, against Luton Town, Clapton moved out again.

PROFESSIONAL FOWL

When Montrose joined the Scottish League in 1929, they discovered that chickens were wandering into the ground and damaging the pitch.

FOREST FIRE

On 24 August 1968, Nottingham Forest's main stand caught fire during the First Division game with Leeds. The 34,000 crowd were evacuated by police but the stand was gutted. Forest were forced to play their remaining fixtures that year at neighbours Notts County.

THE GREEN PARTY

Luton Town's first game at Kenilworth Road, in 1905, was known as "The Green Game". Opponents Plymouth Argyle played in green, the referee's surname was Green and the match was kicked off by a local brewer by the name of Green.

WHEN THE LIGHTS GO OUT

When the floodlights failed midway through the second half of the Fourth Division game between Watford and Shrewsbury in April 1959, spectators at Vicarage Road set fire to newspapers in an attempt to provide sufficient light for the game to continue. Both teams scored in this uneasy gloom but, with Shrewsbury leading 5–2, the referee called the game off 14 minutes from time. Shrewsbury won the rearranged fixture 4–1 to clinch promotion to Division Three.

ASSETS FROZEN

With match after match postponed during the "Big Freeze" of 1963 and therefore no revenue coming in, hard-up Halifax Town opened The Shay to the paying public as a skating rink.

KICKING UP A STINK

The name of Aberdeen's ground, Pittodrie, is Gaelic for "dunghill".

GROUNDS FOR CELEBRATION

Wolves are the only club to have appeared in FA Cup Finals at five different grounds – Kennington Oval, Fallowfield, Crystal Palace, Stamford Bridge and Wembley.

BOMBED OUT

Only one Football League ground was hit by German bombs during both World Wars – Hartlepool. The club's repeated claims for compensation from the German government fell on deaf ears.

SPOT THE BULL

When fans invaded the Raith Rovers pitch during a

match in 1887, the ground's owner, Robert Stark, dispersed them by unleashing a bull he kept tethered in an adjacent field.

NO NEAR NEIGHBOURS

Carlisle United's Brunton Park ground is the most isolated League venue in Britain. It is 58 miles from its nearest Football League neighbour – Newcastle United – and is actually closer to a Scottish club, Queen of the South, who play in Dumfries.

NEAREST AND DEAREST

The two closest League grounds in Britain are Dens Park and Tannadice in Dundee. They are just 200 yards apart along the same street. In England, Nottingham Forest and Notts County are separated by little more than the River Trent.

BY THE SEA

The nearest British League ground to the sea is Arbroath's Gayfield. It stands just over 50 yards from the water. The closest to a day at the seaside in England is Grimsby Town's Blundell Park which is about 150 yards from the sea.

MISLEADING NAME

The British League ground which is farthest from a railway station is Forfar Athletic's ironically named Station Park. It is 14 miles from the nearest stations at Dundee and Arbroath.

EYE LEVEL

Aberdeen were the first club in Britain to introduce dugouts. Their manager Donald Coleman suggested them so that he could better study the players' footwork.

BATHING BOOTIES

When Grimsby Town used to play at Clee Park, the players had to get changed in bathing-huts which were wheeled up from the beach.

BACK TO GRASS

Preston North End were the last Football League club to play on an artificial pitch. They finally converted Deepdale back to grass in the summer of 1994.

A SMASHING TIME

Arbroath switched on their new floodlights with a game against Dundee United in 1955, only for one of the lamps to be smashed by a hefty clearance from an Arbroath player.

GYPSY CURSE

When Derby County's old home, the Baseball Ground, was built on the site of an old gypsy encampment in 1895, the gypsies were said to have placed a curse on the club. Over the next nine years, the Rams reached the FA Cup semi-finals seven times, progressing to the final itself on three occasions. But not once did they lift the trophy. The hoodoo lingered on until 1946 when, before the final with Charlton, Derby captain Jack Nicholas asked some gypsies to lift the curse. Suddenly Derby's luck changed and they took the trophy for the first time, 4–1.

THE BARD OF BLUNDELL PARK

A call came over the Grimsby Town loudspeaker in 1993: "Would the owner of a yellow Landcruiser 777 Romeo Romeo . . . " The announcement brought a lusty chorus from the stand of "Wherefore art thou Romeo?" Just then the Grimsby substitute began to warm up. It was Craig Shakespeare.

8

CRAZY KEEPERS

NEV'S SIT-IN

Transfer-seeking Everton keeper Neville Southall staged a half-time protest during the game with Leeds on 25 August 1990. While his team-mates were in the dressing-room, Southall sat silently on the pitch at the foot of a goalpost.

FAT BOY'S LIMB

The heaviest player in the history of professional football was William "Fatty" Foulke who kept goal for Sheffield United, Chelsea, Bradford City and England. He was 6 feet 2½ inches tall and, as his career progressed, he expanded from 15 stone to a massive 25 stone. He wore size 12 boots and 24-inch-collar shirts. Such was the strength in his right arm that he could punch the ball to the halfway line. He once stopped a game by snapping the crossbar and, if he was injured, it needed at least six men to carry him off since no stretcher was able to bear his weight. He also had a fearsome temper with an almost pathological dislike for opposing centre-forwards. One who fell foul of him in season 1898–9 was Liverpool's George Allan. In a bizarre incident, Foulke lost his temper, picked Allan up, turned him upside down and stood him on his head in the penalty-area mud. Foulke was hugely aggrieved when the referee awarded a penalty against him.

COMPUTER BLIP

Liverpool goalkeeper David James attributed his loss of form in 1998 to spending too many hours at home playing on computer games.

TALKING BUDGIE

John "Budgie" Burridge was so dedicated to the game during a career which took in the likes of Blackpool, Crystal Palace and Wolves that he used to watch *Match of the Day* in his full goalkeeping kit, complete with jersey, gloves and boots. He was even known to take a ball to bed at night and, much to the alarm of his wife, to conduct an imaginary interview with Gerald Sinstadt in his sleep. Burridge modelled his play on Peter Shilton but carried his admiration to extremes. He once took a photograph of Shilton to his barber so that he could give him the same hairstyle!

WORE COAT IN GOAL

Preston's Welsh international goalkeeper Jimmy

Trainor was such a spectator during his team's 18–0 thrashing of Reading in 1893–4 that when it started to rain in the second half, he put on a raincoat. He only took it off on the two occasions that he was called briefly into action.

FREE-KICK SPECIALIST

Paraguay international goalkeeper Jose Luis Chilavert scored no fewer than eight goals for his club, Velez Sarsfield of Argentina, in 1996. He specialised in going AWOL from his own penalty area and wandering up-field to take free-kicks and penalties. His most spectacular effort was a 60-yard free-kick in a league game against River Plate, taken quickly after he had spotted the opposing keeper German Burgos off his line. The two men met again in a World Cup qualifier in Buenos Aires later that year. This time Chilavert beat Burgos with a free-kick from 25 yards.

PLENTY OF PADDING

Middlesbrough goalkeeper Tim Williamson, who won seven England caps between 1905 and 1913, came up with a cunning plan to make himself look more imposing to forwards. He used to wear several jerseys under his main one so that he all but filled the goal.

SAVED BY THE BELL

Alan Bond, goalkeeper with Gwent amateur side

Newport Civil Service, achieved the distinction of being the first keeper to answer a phone call while facing a penalty. Civil Service were playing local rivals Hamdden in a cup tie when the latter were awarded a penalty. As the Hamdden striker began his run-up, the tense silence was broken by the ringing of Bond's mobile phone which he had left in the corner of the net and had forgotten to switch off. Bond shouted, "Hang on a minute" and answered the call from his babysitter while the Hamdden players looked on in disbelief. On coming off the phone, he was booked by the referee for ungentle-manly conduct. But he had the last laugh. For when the penalty was eventually taken, he saved it.

ALBERT'S ANTICS

Legendary Notts County goalkeeper Albert Iremonger, who played 564 games for the club between 1905 and 1926, used to love arguing with referees. He once irritated the crowd at West Ham to such an extent that a woman marched on to the pitch and hit him with her umbrella. Iremonger was also fond of making sorties from goal to take throw-ins or even corners. In a match against Blackburn he took a penalty, only to see his powerful kick strike the crossbar and bounce back into play, over his head and towards the empty Notts County net. Iremonger turned on his heels and hared back in pursuit of the ball. Racing the speedy Blackburn winger, Iremonger stretched his 6 feet 5½ inch frame and made a desperate lunge to boot the ball away from his opponent. Alas, in doing so, he succeeded in slicing the ball into his own net.

YAKKETY YAK

Manchester United goalkeeper Alex Stepney once dislocated his jaw while shouting at a team-mate.

PYM'S NO. 13

Dick Pym, the Bolton and England keeper of the 1920s, would refuse to travel to an away game if the numbers on his rail ticket added up to 13. Another of his superstitions was to carry a lump of coal in his pocket at all times – even during matches.

THE SCORPION SAVE

Colombian keeper Ren Higuita stunned Wembley in 1995 with his amazing "scorpion" save against England. To keep out a shot from Jamie Redknapp, Higuita did a handstand, arched his back and knocked the ball off the goal-line with the studs of his upturned boots.

LET US PRAY

Isidore Irandir, goalkeeper with Brazilian club Rio Preto, always knelt down in the goalmouth at the start of a match to say his prayers. He went into his routine just as opponents Corinthians kicked off and was still on his knees when a shot from the halfway line by Roberto Rivelino flew past his ears and into the net. As Corinthians celebrated, Irandir's brother ran on to the pitch armed with a revolver and pumped half a dozen bullets into the ball.

9

RED CARD

WHAT'S UP, DOC?

Brazilian striker Edmilson celebrated his goal for Atletico Mineiro in a 1998 League match against America-Belo Horizonte by deliriously eating a carrot on the pitch – in reference to America's nickname, the Rabbits. American midfielder Dinho was then sent off for taking violent revenge. "He didn't see the funny side," said Edmilson. The referee was equally bemused, adding: "What amazed me most was the sweaty taste the carrot must have had – he'd kept it in his shorts for 20 minutes until he scored!"

FIVE OFF

The first time five players were sent off in a Football League match was on 22 February 1997 when two from Chesterfield and three from visitors Plymouth Argyle were ordered off during a Second Division game. Four of the five were dismissed following a last-minute goalmouth brawl. Having waited 109 years for such an incident, the second case of five off in a League match took place just ten months later. On 2 December 1997, in a Second Division match at Wigan, one Wigan player and four from Bristol Rovers received their marching orders.

MASS BRAWL

Bangu took the Brazilian title for the first time in their history in 1967 by defeating Flamengo in Rio de Janeiro. However, as is the custom in South America, the match was not without incident. A total of nine players were sent off – five from Flamengo, four from Bangu – and there was a mass brawl involving photographers, radio commentators and officials.

EARLY BATH

Bologna's Giuseppe Lorenzo set a world record for the fastest sending-off when he was dismissed for striking an opponent after just ten seconds of an Italian League match with Parma on 9 December 1990.

FOUR OFF

Hereford United had four players sent off in the last 18 minutes of their Third Division game with

Northampton on 6 September 1992. Despite finishing the match with only seven men, Hereford held out for a 1–1 draw.

WAGGY'S WOE

Following the introduction of red cards for sending-off offences in Britain, Blackburn Rovers' winger David Wagstaffe had the dubious distinction of being the first player to see red when he was dismissed at Orient on 2 October 1976.

QUICK OFF THE MARK

On 13 March 1994 Crewe goalkeeper Mark Smith went into the record books as the fastest sending-off in British history when he was dismissed after just 19 seconds of the Third Division game at Darlington for hauling down Darlington striker Robbie Painter. The resultant penalty turned out to be the only goal of the game . . . But Sheffield Wednesday keeper Kevin Pressman beat that on 13 August 2000 when he was sent off after just 13 seconds of the Division One game at Wolves for handling the ball outside his area.

BAD START

Graeme Souness was sent off in his first game as player-manager for Rangers in 1986, for a bad foul at

Hibernian. To complete the new boss's misery, Rangers lost 2–1. Another player-manager to be sent off on his debut was Swindon Town's Steve McMahon, at Southend in December 1994.

SILLY BILLY

Oldham left-back Billy Cook refused to leave the field after being sent off in the 55th minute of a game at Middlesbrough in 1915. So referee Mr H. Smith of Nottingham walked off and abandoned the match. Oldham were losing 4–1 at the time and that result stood. Cook was suspended for a year.

HIGGINS' HAWTHORNS HORROR

Tranmere defender Dave Higgins was sent off twice at West Bromwich in the space of 12 days in April 1995. The first occasion was in a reserve match, the second in the course of Rovers' 5–1 League defeat at The Hawthorns.

CELTIC CHAOS

Celtic had four players sent off in a stormy clash with Racing Club of Argentina for the World Club Championship in 1967 but carried on playing with eight men rather than seven because nobody knew exactly who had been sent off.

FEUDING TEAM-MATES

Charlton forwards Derek Hales and Mike Flanagan were sent off for fighting with each other during a third round FA Cup tie with Maidstone United on 9 January 1979. Five years later, Hearts defenders Graeme Hogg and Craig Levein were banned for ten matches by the Scottish FA after they swapped punches during a preseason friendly with Raith Rovers. And in November 1995 Blackburn Rovers' colleagues David Batty and Graeme Le Saux were each suspended for two European games by UEFA after they started brawling with each other in a European Champions' League match with Spartak Moscow.

CARD SHARP

Even though there were only 33 fouls in the entire match, a 1998–9 Spanish League clash between Atletico Madrid and Athletic Bilbao produced 16 yellow cards and two red.

UNUSUAL PROTEST

Piacenza captain Settimo Lucci was sent off during the Serie A clash with Lazio on 27 August 1995 for arguing with the referee over the award of a penalty to his own side! Lucci felt the referee was simply trying to even things up after giving a controversial spot-kick to Lazio two minutes earlier.

TREBLE TROUBLE

Former St Mirren captain Billy Abercrombie was sent off three times in the same match – against Motherwell in 1986. Referee Louis Thow brandished the red card at Abercrombie three times – first for the original offence, the second for talking back and the third for dissent. Abercrombie was banned for 12 matches.

VINNIE IN A HURRY

In his Chelsea days, Vinnie Jones achieved the distinction of being booked after just three seconds. The ball hadn't even left the centre-circle at the start of the fifth round FA Cup tie with visiting Sheffield United in 1992 when Jones went into the referee's notebook for scything down a United player. Vinnie's impetuosity may be explained by the fact that he himself was a former Sheffield United player. Indeed only the previous year Vinnie had set the standard when, playing for United at Maine Road, he was booked after only five seconds for a foul on Manchester City's Peter Reid. After 55 minutes he was booked for a second foul on Reid and sent off.

CLEAN-CUT GARY

Gary Lineker went through his entire career without being booked.

ARGIE BARGIE

Nineteen players were arrested when a 1971 South American (Libertadores) Cup match between Argentinian champions Boca Juniors and Sporting Cristal of Peru erupted into a mass brawl. Three of the 19 were taken to hospital with assorted wounds and the rest were taken to a police station in Buenos Aires. They were all given suspended 30-day jail sentences.

FIERY REPUTATION

Duncan Ferguson's disciplinary record in Scotland was so bad that he used to be known north of the border as "Duncan Disorderly".

WRITER'S CRAMP

At a cup match between Tongham Youth Club of Surrey and Hampshire side Hawley in 1969, the referee ended up booking all 22 players, including one who was carted off to hospital, and one of the linesmen.

MURRAY WALKER

On 31 March 1973 in a Fourth Division game against Doncaster, John Murray of Bury became the first person to score a Football League hat-trick and then have to make the long walk to the dressing-room after being sent off.

SHILTS SENT PACKING

Playing his 971st League game, for Plymouth against Hull on 28 August 1992, Peter Shilton was sent off for the first time in his career.

TRASHED REFEREE'S ROOM

Playing for West Ham, Ian Wright was fined £17,500 and banned for three matches for trashing referee Rob Harris's room after being sent off in the home game with Leeds on 1 May 1999.

SEVEN-MAN STRANRAER

Stranraer became the first Scottish club to have four men sent off in a League fixture when they travelled to Airdrie on 3 December 1994. Stranraer looked set for a rare win when they led 1–0, but by the 59th minute they were down to seven men and finished up losing 8–1. Hearts also had four men sent off – at Rangers in 1996 – as did Albion Rovers at Queen's Park in 1997.

TWENTY OFF

Trouble flared after two Sportivo Ameliano players were

sent off during a Paraguayan League match with General Caballero in May 1993. A ten-minute fight followed, at the end of which referee William Weiler was obliged to dismiss a further 18 players, including the remainder of the Sportivo team. Not surprisingly, the match was abandoned.

ON BEST BEHAVIOUR

Southend United didn't have a single player sent off between 1920 and 1952 – a total of 1027 matches.

RED FOR PEPPER

York City's Nigel Pepper was sent off three times against Darlington in the 1990–1 season – twice in Fourth Division matches and once in an FA Cup tie.

CHRISTMAS JEER

Wrexham's Ambrose Brown was sent off after just 20 seconds of the Third Division (North) match against Hull City on Christmas Day 1936.

WILD WILLIE

Scottish winger Willie Johnston jointly holds the record for the most sendings-off in a career. He was dismissed 21 times – seven for Rangers, six for West

Bromwich Albion, four for Vancouver Whitecaps, three for Hearts and once for Scotland. In September 1976 he was sent off for the tenth time in his career after aiming a kick at the referee during a game with Brighton and was suspended for five months for bringing the game into disrepute. Centre-forward Roy McDonough, who plied his trade with a number of lower division clubs in the Eighties and Nineties, was also sent off 21 times – 13 in the Football League and eight in non-League.

SACKED AT HALF-TIME

Leyton Orient sacked defender Terry Howard at half-time during their Second Division game with Blackpool on 7 February 1995. Howard was making his 397th appearance for the club but his first-half performance was described by the O's management as "unacceptable". Howard was fined two weeks' wages and given a free transfer.

MATCH FIXER

Enoch West of Manchester United was banned for life after being found guilty, with others, of fixing the result of a match between United and Liverpool on 2 April 1915. But whereas the others had their bans lifted after the First World War, on account of their distinguished war records, West's remained in place until 1945, by which time he was 62 and too old to play.

GENTLEMAN JIM

Defender Jimmy Dickinson made 764 League appearances for Portsmouth between 1946 and 1965. Throughout his illustrious career, he was never cautioned or even warned by a referee.

RECORD BROKEN

When Frank Saul was sent off for Spurs at Burnley on 4 December 1965, he became the first Spurs player to be dismissed in a League game for 37 years.

PIG SICK

Footballer Dave Clark, a butcher by trade, was banned from playing for Worthing United in 1997 after nailing a pig's head to the opposition dug-out before a game.

TEN BOOKED

Denied victory by a hotly disputed, last-gasp penalty in a second round FA Cup tie at Crystal Palace in 1962, Mansfield Town players were so angry that they gave the referee the slow handclap as he left the field. He promptly booked all ten of them, the only one to escape being goalkeeper Colin Treharne who was still picking the ball out of the net. Mansfield's frustration subsided when they won the replay 7–2.

HARD-MAN HURLOCK

Fulham midfielder Terry Hurlock was suspended for a total of 15 games in 1994–5 as he became the first player to reach 61 disciplinary points in a season.

BEN'S BAN

Exeter City substitute Ben Rowe was sent off for dissent against Fulham on 27 October 1990 while still sitting in the dug-out.

CAMERA SHY

Argentine World Cup goalkeeper Ubaldo Fillol was given a five-day suspended sentence in 1978 for assaulting a photographer. The press man fell foul of Fillol after the keeper had been sent off for kicking an opposing forward.

LATIN PUNCH-UP

The South American Super Cup quarter-final between Gremio of Brazil and Penarol of Uruguay in 1993 descended into chaos when eight players were sent off – four from each side.

COOL IT

When Manchester City's Mike Doyle and Manchester United's Lou Macari refused to leave the pitch after being sent off in a March 1974 derby at Old Trafford, Welsh referee Clive "the book" Thomas decided to take both teams off for a ten-minute cooling down period. After the pair finally agreed to go, the match was resumed and ended in a goalless draw.

PUT HIS FOOT DOWN

Barcelona forward Hristo Stoichkov was banned for six months in 1990 for stamping on the referee's foot after being sent off during a Spanish Supercup tie against Real Madrid.

LEADING BY EXAMPLE

Having seen three of his players sent off in the first 38 minutes of an FA Cup second qualifying round match at Staines in 1989, Dunstable player/manager Kevin Millett elected to lead his players off. With Dunstable losing 1–0 at the time, the match was abandoned. Millet, in his first season as manager, said afterwards:

"In retrospect, I think it was a bad decision to take the team off but the whole thing was getting out of hand. I could see another two or three of them getting sent off."

NOT SO CLEVER, TREVOR

Trevor Hockey became the first Welsh international to be sent off when he was dismissed during his country's 3–0 defeat in Poland in 1973.

FIVE OFF IN GOAL DISPUTE

The most explosive start to a match was the Brazilian Cup clash between America Tres Rios and Itaperuna. Five America Tres Rios players were ordered off in the first ten minutes after protesting too vehemently about the award of a goal to Itaperuna. The referee quickly abandoned the match and the tie was awarded to Itaperuna.

FIVE DISMISSALS IN A SEASON

In 1987–8, Dave Caldwell was sent off a record five times in one season – twice for Chesterfield and three times for Torquay United.

CHEWED NOTEBOOK

After being cautioned for swearing during a Bristol Suburban League match in 1983, Mike Bagley of Ibstock Cattybrook FC snatched the referee's notebook and started chewing it. Seeing this, the ref promptly sent him off.

ENGLAND SHAME

Alan Mullery was the first England player to be sent off when he was ordered off against Yugoslavia in a European Championship match in Florence on 5 June 1968.

POLICE CAUTION

The Third Division game between Colchester and Millwall on 13 September 1980 was held up for three minutes when Police Sergeant Frank Ruggles marched on to the pitch to tick off Millwall defender Mel Blyth for swearing. Blyth, who had been directing his venom at his team-mates, was lectured at length by the Sergeant. As tempers became heated, the referee had to intervene to keep the two men apart. Blyth escaped with a caution after the incident – the first-known instance of a police officer invading the pitch.

PULLED GUN ON MANAGER

Frank Barson, a fiery centre-half who played for a

number of clubs between the wars, was sent off and suspended on a number of occasions. But that was nothing compared to what happened during his time at Aston Villa when he was said to have reacted so angrily to his latest punishment that he pulled a gun on the manager.

THE HITMAN AND HARE

Barcelona's volatile Bulgarian striker Hristo Stoichkov was sent off in the 90th minute of a Spanish League game with Atletico Madrid in the spring of 1994 . . . because a hare had run on to the Nou Camp pitch. Barcelona were leading 5–3 and Stoichkov, already on a yellow card, was shaping up for a hat-trick. But just as he prepared to shoot, the errant hare collided with an Atletico defender and the referee immediately brought play to a halt. Stoichkov blew his top at the ref and was sent off. The hare was killed.

CROWE GETS THE BIRD

Arsenal's Jason Crowe was sent off after just 33 seconds of his first-team debut. No sooner had he come on as a substitute during the third round Coca-Cola Cup tie with Birmingham City on 14 October 1997 than he was on his way back to the dressing-room.

MASCOT SENT OFF

The Macclesfield Town mascot was sent off for making

inflammatory gestures during a players' brawl in a match against Lincoln in 1998. Two Lincoln players were also sent off.

BARE-FACED CHEEK

Arsenal full-back Sammy Nelson was suspended by the club for two weeks and fined two weeks' wages for lowering his shorts and baring his backside to the Highbury crowd after scoring the Gunners' equaliser in a 1–1 draw with Coventry in April 1979. Nelson had put through his own goal in the first half.

UNHOLY ROW

A boys' church club football final in Glasgow in 1964 was abandoned after half an hour when it erupted into a free-for-all involving spectators. The trouble in the match between St John's and St Joseph's started when a boy who had been sent off refused to go. As onlookers began trading punches, the police were called in to disperse rival factions.

10

GREAT SCOTS

STRUCK DOWN

On 1 April 2000, Hamilton Academicals players went on strike and refused to play in a Second Division game at Stenhousemuir. The match was postponed and the Scottish League deducted 15 points from Accies' total, which was sufficient to consign them to relegation.

WALK-OUT

At the start of the 1972–73 season, 16 Falkirk players walked out after the club said it would no longer pay travelling expenses or for players' lunches.

JOY AT LAST

On 2 April 1994, Cowdenbeath beat Arbroath 1–0 to end a two-year run of 38 home League matches without a win.

BUSY KEEPER

In 1931–2, Edinburgh City conceded 146 goals in 38 League games – nearly four goals a game.

POSITIONAL SWITCH

Former Rangers and Scotland goalkeeper Andy Goram played as a centre-forward at school.

KILLIE CHAOS

The very first Scottish Cup tie took place in October 1873 between Kilmarnock and Renton. Unfortunately the Kilmarnock players weren't too sure of the rules of soccer and kept confusing it with rugby, giving away endless free-kicks as a result of picking the ball up with their hands. Not surprisingly, they lost 3–0.

FERGIE'S FAREWELL

As a player, Alex Ferguson's last match for Rangers was the 1969 Scottish FA Cup Final against Celtic. Rangers lost 4–0 and their manager David White blamed centre-forward Ferguson for Celtic's first goal, headed in by centre-half Billy McNeill from a corner. Ferguson was supposed to have been marking McNeill.

BERWICK'S FINEST HOUR

The biggest shock in the history of the Scottish FA Cup was Rangers' 1–0 defeat to Berwick Rangers in 1967. Berwick's defiant goalkeeper that day was Jock Wallace who later went on to manage Rangers.

SELL OUT

A total of 146,433 spectators watched the 1937 Scottish FA Cup Final between Celtic and Aberdeen at Hampden Park. And it is estimated that a further 20,000 were locked out of the ground.

STANDING ROOM ONLY

Those who set off early for the vital Second Division basement battle between East Stirlingshire and Leith on 15 April 1939 need not have bothered. For only 32 spectators turned up – the lowest attendance for a senior League game in Britain.

HEARTS PIPPED

Hearts haven't won the Scottish League title since 1960 but they have come agonisingly close on two occasions. In 1965, the race was between them and Kilmarnock and the two teams met on the final day at Tynecastle.

Hearts were two points clear and so needed only a draw to take the championship. But they lost 2–0 and missed the title by one goal. If they had lost 2–1 or 1–0, they would still have been champions, but under the system of goal average, Kilmarnock's 62–33 beat Hearts' 90–49 by 0.042 goals. Six years later the Scottish FA decided to change the calculation for future seasons to goal difference, a system under which Hearts would have comfortably taken the title. Hearts suffered another last-day disaster in 1986. They went into the final round of matches unbeaten in 32 League and Cup games, two points ahead of Celtic and with a four-goal advantage in goal difference. Yet while Celtic were romping home 5–0 at St Mirren, Hearts contrived to concede two goals in the last eight minutes at Dundee and lost 2–0. Suddenly Celtic had a three-goal better difference and the title was theirs. To add insult to injury, a week later Hearts were beaten by Aberdeen in the Scottish Cup Final.

BAD FEELING

After losing 1–0 to Rangers in an 1875 Scottish FA Cup tie, Third Lanark had the result declared invalid because Rangers had kicked off to start both halves. The SFA ordered the match to be replayed and this time Third Lanark won 2–1. Now it was Rangers' turn to protest. They claimed that the Third Lanark goalkeeper's plain clothes made it impossible to distinguish him from the spectators behind the goal and, for good measure, that the crowd ran on to the pitch, causing the game to finish seven minutes early. However, Rangers' appeal was rejected.

PIONEERING HIBS

Hibernian are responsible for three innovations in Scottish football. In the late Seventies, they became the first Scottish club to wear a sponsor's name on their shirts; in 1980 they were the first Scottish club to install undersoil heating; and in 1983 theirs was the first Scottish ground to boast an electronic scoreboard. Back in 1956, they had also been the first Scottish club to play in the European Cup and reached the semi-finals that year before going out to the French team, Stade de Reims.

RENEWED ACQUAINTANCES

Falkirk's appearance in the 1997 Scottish FA Cup Final was their first for 40 years. And, as on the previous occasion, their opponents were Kilmarnock. But whereas Falkirk won in 1957, Kilmarnock gained their revenge with a 1–0 victory.

KEEPERS ON THE MARK

Both goalkeepers – Jimmy Brownlie of Third Lanark and Clem Hampton of Motherwell – scored when the two teams met in a Scottish Division One game in 1910.

WHO'S A PRETTY BOY THEN?

East Stirling started out as a Falkirk cricket club called

Bainsford Bluebonnets. Wisely they changed their name to Bainsford Britannia.

THE FOUR ORIGINALS

Only four clubs have enjoyed continuous membership of the Scottish League since its formation in 1890 – Celtic, Hearts, Rangers and St Mirren.

THE RONNIE

As a schoolboy, Ronnie Corbett had a trial with Hearts but was rejected because he was too small.

A QUESTION OF GOALS

Ally McCoist became the first player to score 200 goals in the Scottish Premier Division when he scored Rangers' winner at Falkirk on 12 December 1992.

DOUBLE DATE

On 16 February 1993, goalkeeper Scott Howie helped Scotland's Under-21 team to a 3–0 victory over Malta before turning out later that same day for Clyde in a First Division fixture against Queen of the South.

LUCKY CHARM

Following his arrival from Motherwell in 1972, Tom Forsyth played 29 games in domestic competition for Rangers before finishing on the losing side.

GLASGOW RIOT

Following two draws between Rangers and Celtic in the final of the 1909 Scottish FA Cup, the crowd were baying for extra time. However, the rules stated that extra time could be played only after a third match and so as the players left the field, the frustrated spectators rioted. As a result of the mayhem, both teams refused to play a third game and the Scottish FA withheld the trophy.

DUNDEE SHAKER

Berwick Rangers shook First Division Dundee in the third round of the Scottish FA Cup in 1954 with a 3–0 victory. Berwick finished sixth in Division "C" that season. In second place in the table were Dundee Reserves!

STILL WAITING

Apart from the two new teams – Elgin City and Peter-head – the only current clubs never to have won a divisional title in the Scottish League are Arbroath and Stenhousemuir. Both joined the League in 1922.

JAKE'S PROGRESS

Sacked as manager of Forfar Athletic in 1969–70, Jake Young turned out in a trial match for Arbroath Reserves and was promptly signed by the Gayfield club as a player.

BARREN RUN ENDED

Rangers' victory in the 1970 Scottish League Cup Final brought them their first silverware for five long years. And when Partick Thistle shook Celtic in the final of the same competition two years later, it was the Jags' first trophy in over half a century.

OPTIMISTIC BID

In 1980 little Dumbarton (average gate around 900) launched a surprise bid for the great Johann Cruyff. Manager Sean Fallon said: "Lots of people think we are a small club but we set our sights high. Nothing ventured, nothing gained is my motto." However, Fallon did acknowledge that Cruyff probably had other offers to consider.

THE REF WAS BLIND!

Having been beaten by Vale of Leven in an early Scottish FA Cup tie, Hearts protested about the result "on account of the utter incapability of the referee owing to a physical infirmity of defective eyesight". The referee duly produced a medical certificate from an eye specialist and Hearts were made to apologise.

PRIESTLY PERK

Celtic used to allow priests and women into matches at Parkhead for free.

OVER-CONFIDENT

Kilmarnock were so confident of winning the 1957 Scottish FA Cup Final against Falkirk that they had already arranged a civic reception to celebrate their triumph. But all they could eat was humble pie as Falkirk won 2–1 after a replay.

GOAL GLUT

In the course of season 1912–13, every member of Greenock Morton's first-team squad found their way on to the scoresheet – the first British club to achieve that particular goal.

UNLUCKY JIM

Playing his very last game before retirement, veteran Aberdeen goalkeeper Jim Leighton broke his jaw in the third minute of the 2000 Scottish FA Cup Final with Rangers after diving at the feet of Rod Wallace. With Leighton being stretchered off, Aberdeen had no substitute keeper and, with striker Robbie Winters taking over between the posts, slumped to a 4–0 defeat. Rangers' victory allowed them to complete their fifth League and Cup double in the space of nine years.

JUST THE TICKET

Cowdenbeath were saved from extinction in 1909 by the staging of a whippet race at their grounds to raise much needed revenue. The club was also helped by benevolent railway officials who let the players travel on trains to away games without tickets.

NERVOUS WRECKS

On their way to the Canary Islands for an overseas tour in 1930, Raith Rovers were shipwrecked when their ship capsized.

STOP-GAP

Berwick Rangers' physiotherapist Bobby Gordon was forced to play in goal for the first six minutes of their match with Albion Rovers in 1987–8 after the goal-keeper's car had broken down on the way to the game.

DIS-GUSTED

The quickest abandonment on record must be in the Scottish Premier Reserve League game between Dundee United and Dunfermline at Arbroath on 26 February 1998. The match was called off after just 90 seconds' play because of high winds. Pity the poor fans who turned up to watch.

BRECHIN BLITZED

Brechin City suffered three 10–0 defeats during the 1937–8 season – to Airdrie, Albion Rovers and Cow-denbeath.

FIXTURE JAM

Broxburn and Beith met five times in a first round Scottish FA Cup tie in 1909, the last three games being played on three consecutive days. Beith finally won 4–2 on a Friday and then had to meet St Mirren in the second round the following day. The strain of playing four games in four days proved too much for Beith who went down 3–0.

OLD FIRM MONOPOLY

When Third Lanark took the Scottish League title in 1904, it would be the last time for 28 years that it would be won by any club other than Rangers or Celtic. And when Alex Ferguson led Aberdeen to the League title in 1980, it was the first time for 15 years that the championship had gone outside Glasgow.

IF AT FIRST . . .

On 22 February 1979, Falkirk finally beat Inverness Thistle in the Scottish FA Cup after a record 29 postponements. The tie had originally been scheduled for 6 January.

DANNY BOY

When East Fife played Kilmarnock in the 1938 Scottish FA Cup Final, they had to borrow Danny McKerrall, a Falkirk reserve, just for the game because their regular left-winger was injured and they had nobody to play in that position. Not only was McKerrall's only Scottish Cup tie a final but he collected a winners' medal and scored two crucial goals as East Fife became the only Second Division side ever to lift the trophy.

VALE OF GLOOM

Clyde were the first team to notch double figures in the

Scottish League when they crushed Vale of Leven 10–3 on 15 August 1891.

LAST STRAW FOR HAY

St Mirren boss David Hay was so furious with his team after their 5–0 home defeat at the hands of Celtic in 1991 that he announced that he was withholding the players' wages.

SIZE MATTERS

After Rangers lost 4–3 at Arbroath in the 1884–5 Scottish FA Cup, they complained that the pitch wasn't wide enough. Sure enough, when it was measured it was found to be 11 inches short. The tie was replayed five weeks later and this time Rangers won 8–1.

QUICK STARTER

On his debut for Dundee against Rangers in 1984, Colin Harris scored his first goal with his first touch in the first minute.

A MAN FOR ALL POSITIONS

In his 20 years with the club between 1910 and 1930, James Gordon played in every position for Rangers, including goalkeeper.

11

UPS AND DOWNS

UNITED'S DEBT TO LIONS

Manchester United were saved from relegation to the financial wilderness of the Third Division (North) in 1933–4 thanks to a last-day victory at Millwall. At the start of the day, United were languishing in 21st place, a point behind Millwall, but a 2–0 victory at The Den enabled them to preserve their Second Division status at the expense of the South London club. History almost repeated itself in 1989–90, this time in the old First Division. Manager Alex Ferguson was under fire and United appeared to be in freefall until they visited The Den to take on struggling Millwall. At the time it was seen as a six-pointer in the relegation stakes. United fought back from a goal down to win 2–1 and have never looked back. Millwall were relegated.

THE GREAT ESCAPE

Goalkeeper Jimmy Glass became a footballing legend on 8 May 1999 by scoring the goal which kept Carlisle

United in the Football League. With just seconds remaining of the final match of the season, against Plymouth, the scores were level. Carlisle needed a victory to preserve their League status and so, in one last act of desperation, Glass went up for a corner kick. When the kick came over, a rebound landed at his feet and he lashed the ball into the net for the winner. There were just ten seconds left on the clock. Carlisle's relief meant misery for Scarborough who were relegated to the Conference. Scarborough had been held that day by Peterborough and, coincidentally, a year later Peterborough again saved Carlisle from relegation to the Conference on the final day of the season. For while Carlisle were losing at Brighton, they stayed up thanks to Peterborough's victory at Chester.

CITY SLACKERS

Bristol City became the first Football League club to be relegated in three successive seasons when they plunged from First to Fourth Division between 1980 and 1982. Wolves then repeated the feat between 1984 and 1986.

THE LATE SHOW

Trying to reach the top two flights for the first time in their history, Gillingham were leading Manchester City 2–0 in the 1998–9 Second Division play-off final with barely a minute left. But City scored twice to force extra time and penalties, which Gillingham lost. The Gills were back at Wembley for the play-off final the following year, but this time it was they who scored two late goals to overhaul Wigan Athletic 3–2 and finally make it to the First Division.

BRIDGING THE GAP

In 1971–2, Huddersfield Town were playing in the First Division while Hereford United were in the Southern League. Yet two seasons later, the clubs met in the Third Division, Huddersfield having been relegated twice and Hereford being elected to the Football League and winning promotion at the first attempt.

HUNG OVER

As the 1908–9 season drew to a close, Leicester Fosse were already doomed to relegation from the First Division and Nottingham Forest were in grave danger of joining them. But Forest managed to save their skin by thumping Fosse 12–0. Suspicious of what was then a record score for Division One and between near neighbours, a Football League Commission launched an inquiry into the circumstances surrounding the match. But far from uncovering any hint of bribery, the Commission concluded that Fosse's performance was simply down to the fact that they were still hung over from a team-mate's wedding the day before.

BORO ROMP

The 15-point margin by which Middlesbrough won the

Second Division in 1973–4 was the biggest ever by a Football League team under the old system of two points for a win.

UNDER THE INFLUENCE

Shortly before Christmas 1975, Crystal Palace led the Third Division by seven points and manager Malcolm Allison was telling everyone that they were the best team ever to have played at that level. So when hypnotist Ronald Markham – stage name "Romark" – offered his services, the Palace boss didn't think he needed them. Hurt by the rejection, Markham went straight to Gordon Jago, boss of Palace's South London rivals Millwall who were labouring around the middle of the table. Romark not only offered to help Millwall but put a curse on Allison and Palace. Suddenly Millwall hit form at the same time as Palace foundered. At the end of the season, Millwall snatched the third promotion spot behind Hereford and Cardiff while Palace could manage only fifth.

VALE INJUSTICE

Port Vale did everything but win promotion from Division Two in 1993. They finished third in the table with 89 points – the highest total never to earn promotion in any division. And in the play-off final, they lost to West Bromwich Albion – a team they had already beaten twice in the League.

LUCKY ARSENAL

Arsenal were only promoted to the First Division in 1919–20 because of a reorganisation of the League. They had finished fifth in the Second Division in the last season before the war but were invited to step up a division because Division One was being extended from 20 to 22 clubs. They have never been out of the top flight since.

HOT FOR THE DROP

Crystal Palace and Nottingham Forest have both been relegated three times in the Premiership's eight-year history.

A RUB OF THE LINCOLN GREEN

After winning only five League games all season and having gone four months without a victory, Lincoln City won their last six Second Division matches in 1958 to stay up by a point. The clinching game was a 3–1 home success against Cardiff. Two months earlier, Cardiff had been winning 3–0 at Sincil Bank when the match was abandoned due to a blizzard.

CANARIES KNOCKED OFF THEIR PERCH

Norwich City are the only club to have won a major domestic cup and be relegated in the same season. In

1985 they won the Milk Cup (aka the League Cup) but were also relegated to the old Second Division.

RAITH REJECTS

When Raith Rovers won the Scottish First Division title in 1995, two of their players celebrated by throwing their shorts into the crowd because they wanted to keep their shirts for themselves. "It was probably a daft thing to do," said Steve McAnespie. "But there was no way I wanted to subject our fans to my smelly socks, so the shorts were the next best thing."

OVERDUE SUCCESS

Chester were promoted from Division Four in 1975 by virtue of having 0.03 better goal average than Lincoln City. In doing so, Chester became the last of the then Football League clubs to achieve a promotion.

WEDNESDAY'S YO-YO YEARS

In the course of the 1950s, Sheffield Wednesday were promoted four times from Division Two and relegated on three occasions from Division One. Promotion in 1950 was followed by immediate relegation in 1951 but Wednesday bounced back the following year to win the Second Division title. For the next two seasons they hovered dangerously above the relegation zone – ending up 18th and 19th – until finishing 22nd and bottom in 1955. Undeterred, they took the Second Division

Championship again in 1956 and achieved the relative stability of 14th in Division One in 1957. But the next year they finished bottom again, only to win the Second Division title for the third time in seven years in 1959. And whereas the Fifties had been a decade of ups and downs, Wednesday remained in the First Division throughout the Sixties. Mind you, as soon as 1970 dawned, they were relegated again.

MIXED EMOTIONS

Mick Channon and Bob Hatton both topped their division's scoring lists while playing for a team that was relegated. Channon was the First Division's top scorer in 1973–4 even though the Saints finished 20th. And Hatton headed the Second Division list in 1977–8 for a Blackpool side that also finished in the bottom three.

NOT A SHOT ON GOAL

Back in 1898, promotion and relegation between the two divisions of the Football League was decided by a round-robin series of test matches. But the system was changed in favour of automatic promotion and relegation following a dismal clash between Stoke and Burnley. With both teams needing only a draw to finish top of the mini-league and so attain First Division status, neither side made the slightest effort to win the match. There wasn't a shot on goal in the entire 90 minutes and long before the end spectators were demanding their money back.

BORO BONUS

In 1988 Middlesbrough were promoted via the play-offs to Division One – their second successive promotion. This came just two years after the club's very existence had been threatened by the bailiffs.

BLEAK DAYS

Two of the Football League's founder members – Preston North End and Burnley – both dropped into the Fourth Division for the first time in their history in 1985. To add insult to injury, Preston were forced to apply for re-election the following year.

FOURTH TIME LUCKY

After three consecutive defeats in the First Division play-offs, Ipswich Town finally made it fourth year lucky when they reached the Premiership by beating Barnsley 4–2 on 29 May 2000.

WELSH WOE

Cardiff City conceded fewer goals than any other First Division club in 1928–9 yet still finished bottom of the table.

JINX BROKEN

When Leicester City defeated East Midlands rivals Derby County in the 1994 First Division play-off final, it broke their Wembley jinx. For Leicester had lost on all six previous visits there – four FA Cup Finals and in the play-offs of 1992 and 1993.

LAST SURVIVORS

Relegation in 1966 meant that Southend United were the last club to lose continuous membership of Division Three since its formation in 1920.

LAST-MINUTE BLUES

Sheffield United were relegated from the Premiership in 1994 in the final minute of the final game of the season. A draw with Chelsea at Stamford Bridge would have kept United in the top flight at the expense of Ipswich but Mark Stein's 90th-minute goal gave Chelsea a 3–2 victory and condemned United to the First Division.

COVENTRY HANG ON

Only three current Premiership clubs have held unbroken membership of the top division longer than perennial strugglers Coventry City. The Sky Blues have been members of the elite since 1967 – a record surpassed by only Arsenal (1919), Everton (1954) and Liverpool (1962).

SHEPHERD'S DELIGHT

Ernie Shepherd only played 17 League games in season 1948–9. But all three clubs he appeared for – Fulham, West Bromwich Albion and Hull City – were promoted at the end of that campaign.

PALACE PULL THROUGH

In the 1996 First Division play-off final, Crystal Palace went down to a goal from Leicester's Steve Claridge in the last minute of extra time. The following year, the boot was on the other foot as Palace's David Hopkin snatched a last-gasp Wembley winner against Sheffield United to send Palace back into the Premiership.

POMPEY SCRAPE HOME

After the teams had finished level on points, Portsmouth pipped Manchester City for promotion to the First Division in 1926–7 by five-thousandths of a goal.

A BITTER PILL

When Dundee United were relegated from the Scottish Premier Division in 1995, it was the first time they had played outside the top flight since season 1959–60.

ALWAYS THE BRIDESMAID

With only the top team gaining promotion, Plymouth Argyle finished second in Third Division (South) for six consecutive seasons between 1922 and 1927. They finally won the title – and promotion – in 1930.

LATE SURGE

On 1 March 1989, Leyton Orient languished 15th in Division Four. Promotion seemed impossible. But eight wins and a draw in their last nine home games rocketed them up to sixth in the final table and two more home victories in the play-offs secured the club an unlikely place in Division Three.

STROKE OF LUCK FOR BLACK CATS

The biggest Football League attendance for decades – 72,873 – saw Swindon Town defeat Sunderland 1–0 in the Second Division play-off final at Wembley in 1990 to reach the First Division for the first time in the club's history. But a few weeks later, it was Sunderland who were promoted instead, by default. Swindon had been found guilty of "financial irregularities" and were forced to remain in Division Two.

SNAP DECISION

Police dog Bryn was the toast of Torquay in 1987 . . . despite biting one of their players. It was the last week of the season and Torquay knew that defeat would send them into the Conference. After 82 minutes, they were trailing 2–1 to Crewe when Bryn slipped the attentions of his handler, ran on to the pitch and bit Torquay defender Jim McNichol. In the five minutes that had to be added on for McNichol's injury, Torquay equalised and the draw was enough to send Lincoln down instead. Afterwards Torquay chairman Lew Pope promised: "I'm going to buy Bryn the biggest steak in Torquay!"

12

ON THE SPOT

SUFFERING STOKE

During an FA Cup quarter-final with Notts County on 14 February 1891, a Stoke City shot was punched off the line by the Notts full-back with the goalkeeper well beaten. Stoke were awarded a free-kick on the goal-line which the keeper saved easily. Notts won 1–0 but the incident created such controversy that the FA decided to introduce penalties from September that year. Not that it helped Stoke much, for shortly after the new rule was adopted, they were trailing 1–0 to Aston Villa in a League match when they were awarded a penalty two minutes from time. The Villa keeper promptly picked up the ball and booted it out of the ground. By the time it had been found, the referee had blown for full-time. The rule was subsequently amended to allow time to be added on for taking a penalty.

GREAT SCOTT!

In a match at Burnley on 13 February 1909, Grimsby

Town keeper Walter Scott managed to save three out of four penalties that were awarded against his team.

SPOT OF BOTHER

Three different Notts County players missed the same penalty at Portsmouth on 22 September 1973. Kevin Randall's shot was ordered to be retaken because the goalkeeper had moved; Don Masson's effort was ruled out because he had not waited for the referee to blow his whistle; and then Brian Stubbs failed with the third attempt. Nevertheless County won 2–1.

MUTCH REJOICING

The first penalty to be awarded in an FA Cup Final at Wembley was in 1938. George Mutch kept his cool to convert the spot-kick in the last minute of extra time to give Preston a 1–0 victory over Huddersfield. This was Preston's revenge for 16 years earlier. For in 1922, when the Cup Final was played at Stamford Bridge, Huddersfield had beaten Preston 1–0 and then too the only goal of the game had been a penalty.

INVENTIVE CRUYFF

When Ajax were awarded a penalty against Helmond Sports on 6 December 1982, Johan Cruyff decided against taking a direct shot at goal and instead played a one-two with Jesper Olsen before firing past the startled goalkeeper.

PENALTY ACE

Out of some 50 first-team penalties that he has taken, Southampton's Matthew Le Tissier has failed to score on only one occasion. That was when his spot-kick was saved by Nottingham Forest keeper Mark Crossley in a Premier League match at The Dell on 24 March 1993.

CUP CLANGERS

The first man to miss a penalty in an FA Cup Final was Aston Villa's Charlie Wallace who shot wide in the 1913 final with Sunderland. The miss didn't prove costly as Villa still won 1–0. But it was a different story in 1988 when Liverpool's John Aldridge became the first person to miss a spot-kick in an FA Cup Final at Wembley. His effort was saved by Wimbledon's Dave Beasant and the Dons held on for a famous single-goal victory.

DISSENT QUELLED BY FORCE

Cameroon soldiers rushed on to the pitch and beat up the Congolese national team after they had protested about the award of an 84th-minute penalty against them. Congo had been leading Cameroon 2–1 in the 1976 clash at Brazzaville.

SLOUGH OF DESPOND

Alan Slough scored a hat-trick of penalties for Peterborough United at Chester in 1978 but still finished on the losing side. Chester won the Third Division game 4–3.

PENALTY HERO

Outfield player Eric Viscaal was forced to take over in goal for Belgian team AA Gent against Lokeren in 1994 when Gent's keeper was sent off five minutes from time. The first thing he did was save a Lokeren penalty and then, when Gent were awarded a penalty in the dying seconds, Viscaal ran upfield to score from the spot.

A SURE BET

When Kidderminster Harriers were awarded a penalty against Oldham Athletic in their first round FA Cup tie on 17 January 1907, the referee placed the ball on the spot but then noticed that there was nobody in the Oldham goal. It turned out that the Oldham keeper, Hewitson, was behind the goal among the fans, laying odds that Harriers wouldn't score. He was right too – they didn't. In fact it was a miserable day for Harriers all round as they lost 5–0.

HARD TO BEAT

Ipswich Town goalkeeper Paul Cooper established a

reputation for saving penalties in the Seventies. In 1979–80, he saved eight of the ten penalties he faced. Another keeper who had a knack of saving penalties was Notts County's Roy Brown who stopped six in a row in 1972–3. More recently, Mark Bosnich saved five in two consecutive matches for Aston Villa. He stopped three in the penalty shoot-out at the end of the Coca-Cola Cup semi-final with Tranmere on 26 February 1994. Then on 2 March, he saved two more penalties in a Premiership game at Tottenham.

PENALTY BLITZ

A record five penalties were awarded by referee Kelvin Morton in the Second Division game between Crystal Palace and Brighton on 27 March 1989, including a spell of three in five minutes. Palace managed to miss three of their four but still won 2–1.

FLYING START

On 27 December 1980, Birmingham City goalkeeper Tony Coton saved a Sunderland penalty after just 80 seconds of his full debut. Birmingham won 3–2.

SHOOT-OUT DREAD

Italy have been knocked out on penalties in three successive World Cups.

LANCASHIRE HOTCH-POTCH

Ipswich were awarded three penalties in the second leg of their First Division play-off semi-final against Bolton at Portman Road on 17 May 2000. They scored two and missed one but still emerged 5–3 winners, their cause helped by the sending-off of two Bolton players.

SHRIMPERS COULDN'T FIND THE NET

When Southend United failed to score from a penalty against Wolves in a Second Division match on 28 September 1991, it was the seventh successive penalty they had missed.

QUICK PENALTY

Sammy Collins scored from the penalty spot after a mere ten seconds of Torquay United's Third Division (South) match with Walsall on 29 August 1956. The feat was equalled north of the border on 19 November 1988 by Partick Thistle's Gerry McCoy. He also successfully converted a spot-kick after ten seconds of the First Division game with Ayr United.

GOALSCORING KEEPER

Chesterfield goalkeeper Arthur Birch scored five times for Chesterfield in 1923–4 season – all from penalties.

SHAKY DEBUT

Ipswich Town goalkeeper Richard Wright gave away two penalties on his England debut in Malta on 3 June 2000. Fortunately he saved one and England edged home 2–1.

PRINCE OF WAILS

The First Division title has never been won by a Welsh club, but it was a close-run thing in 1924. In the last minute of the final match of the season, Cardiff City were drawing 0–0 at Birmingham when they were awarded a penalty. All the Welshmen needed to do was score and they would pip Huddersfield for the title. But Len Davies took the kick and missed, and Cardiff lost out on goal average.

CITY BLUES

Manchester City missed three penalties in a First Division game against Newcastle in 1912.

WASTED EFFORT

Two village teams taking part in a West Country cup in 1998–9 fought out a protracted penalty shoot-out before realising that the competition rules required a replay first. With the scores locked at 2–2 after extra time, Morwenstow and Dolton took 22 penalties before Morwenstow prevailed, only to learn that their efforts had been in vain. Fortunately for Morwenstow, they won the replay 2–1.

FIRST SHOOT-OUT

On 5 August 1970, Manchester United beat Hull City 4–3 on penalties in the pre-season Watney Cup after drawing 1–1 – the first time a penalty shoot-out had been used to decide the outcome of a competitive match between two senior British clubs.

DILLON THE HAPPY BUNNY

Portsmouth missed nine penalties in 1982–3 season before Kevin Dillon broke the jinx by scoring twice from the spot against Reading over Easter. In 1986, Dillon became one of the few players to score a hat-trick of penalties in a game when he successfully converted three spot-kicks against Millwall in a Full Members Cup tie at Fratton Park.

SPOT ON

In 1971–2, Manchester City's Francis Lee converted a record 13 penalties in the First Division.

EXTENDED SHOOT-OUT

It needed 44 penalties to settle a shoot-out at the end of

an Argentina League game between Argentinos Juniors and Racing Club on 20 November 1988. Argentinos eventually won 20–19.

PAID THE PENALTY

Penalties were the downfall of little Forfar Athletic in a Scottish FA Cup quarter-final with Dundee United in 1987. Forfar were leading 2–1 at Tannadice when they gave away a last-gasp penalty which United converted to snatch a draw. Then midway through the first half of the replay, Forfar contrived to miss two penalties within the space of a minute. United profited from the let-off to score twice for a 2–0 victory.

ICE-COOL ALEX

Goalkeeper Alex Stepney was Manchester United's joint top scorer for two months in 1973–4, having converted two early-season penalties.

DOUBLE KO

In an FA Cup fifth qualifying round tie against Metro-gas in 1921, Norwich City full-back Benny Smith struck a penalty with such force that it knocked out the opposing keeper Leach. This left Smith to knock the rebound into the empty net. Poor Leach was carried off and his team were also knocked out 2–1.

TAKE SEVEN . . .

Visitors Kilmarnock had to take the same penalty seven times at Partick Thistle in 1945. It was eventually saved and Thistle went on to win 5–3.

13

BARMY ARMIES

CHEESE CRACKERS

Brentford fans adopted cheese as their lucky omen in 1996. For a fourth round FA Cup tie at Charlton, Bees' fans hired a boat to ferry an 80-strong party and pounds of cheese along the Thames to The Valley. "It started as a joke in the second round against Bournemouth," explained Billy Grant of the Brentford Official Unofficial Supporters' Posse. "But then we won – a clear omen. So for the next Cup game at Norwich everyone spontaneously brought along cheese and crackers." Alas, just when Brentford needed a slice of good fortune, the magic of the cheese started to grate and Charlton ran out the 3–2 winners.

CELERY SEARCH

Fans entering Gillingham's Priestfield Stadium in 1996 were subjected to celery searches. As a result of a craze for waving sticks of celery while chanting an obscene song, anyone caught in possession of the vegetable ran the risk of a life ban from the ground.

SEAGULL DROPS 'EM

Scarborough apologised to Brentford in 1998 after the Yorkshire club's mascot, Sammy the Seagull, had mooned at visiting fans.

WHAT A DRAG!

Five Newport County supporters were arrested in 1989 after they turned up for a match at Kidderminster Harriers in drag. A total of 40 County fans had trooped into an Oxfam shop before the game and bought women's clothes.

BIZARRE MISSILE

In March 1999 a disgruntled Manchester City fan threw an asthma inhaler on to the Maine Road pitch during a disappointing draw with Northampton.

WINGS CLIPPED

Swansea mascot Cyril the Swan was banished to the back of the grandstand by the Welsh FA after being found guilty of inciting trouble during the club's FA Cup tie with visiting Millwall in 1998.

I WANNA KISS THE REF

After scoring only two goals in the League before Christmas in the 1994–5 season, Arbroath suddenly hit form with a 5–2 victory over high-flying East Stirlingshire. When his side's fifth goal went in, Arbroath supporter Sye Webster was so excited that he rushed on to the pitch and kissed the referee. But the club took a dim view of his behaviour and banned him from Gayfield for 12 months.

FLAT CAP TRIBUTE

Port Vale fans donned flat caps and marched half a mile to Vale Park for the First Division game with Huddersfield on 6 February 1999 in tribute to recently sacked manager John Rudge, acclaimed as the best boss in the club's history. The flat cap was Rudge's trademark.

ACTION MAN

In 1994 Portsmouth fan Mike Hall announced that he was suing the Endsleigh League in the small claims court for his ticket money and travel costs for what he claimed was a wasted trip to see Pompey beaten by Oldham as a result of two hotly disputed penalties.

GROOM'S GETAWAY

Sunderland fan Stephen Jones deserted his new bride to watch Sunderland beat Grimsby Town 3–0 in 1998–9.

Jones left his wedding reception at Wingate, Co. Durham, and ordered the limousine chauffeur to drive him, his best man and the ushers to The Stadium of Light. Another 28 guests followed behind in a mini-bus. He returned to the reception – and his understanding bride – after the game.

CITY STAMP ON FOWL PLAY

In 1995 a Manchester City fan was banned from bringing dead chickens into the Maine Road ground. He used to celebrate a City goal by swinging the lifeless bird around his head.

MR BEAN GETS A TATTOO

Actor Sean Bean is such a fanatical Sheffield United supporter that he has a tattoo on his arm bearing the legend "100 per cent Blades". This caused problems for the costume department when he was filming the period drama *Sharpe.*

CELEBRITY FANS

Other celebrity fans include: Stuart Adamson (Dunfermline Athletic), Donna Air, Ant and Dec, Tony Blair, John McCririck and Sting (Newcastle United), John Alderton (Hull City), Clive Anderson, Jeremy Beadle and Alan Davies (Arsenal), Jeffrey Archer (Bristol Rovers), Nick Berry and John Cleese (West Ham United), Dickie Bird and Michael Parkinson (Barnsley),

Jim Bowen and Jack Straw (Blackburn Rovers), Jo Brand, Eddie Izzard and Neil Morrissey (Crystal Palace), Gordon Brown (Raith Rovers), Lord Melvyn Bragg (Carlisle United), Emma Bunton and Simon Mayo (Tottenham Hotspur), David Byrne of Talking Heads and Hazel Irvine (Dumbarton), Nicky Campbell and Stephen Hendry (Hearts), Jasper Carrott (Birmingham City), Willie Carson (Swindon Town), Jon Champion (York City), The Chuckle Brothers (Rotherham United), Martin Clunes (Queens Park Rangers), Brian Conley (Watford), Sean Connery and Sharleen Spiteri (Celtic), Elvis Costello and Sue Johnston (Liverpool), Steve Cram (Sunderland), Jim Davidson and Steve Rider (Charlton Athletic), Cat Deeley and Frank Skinner (West Bromwich Albion), Jack Docherty and John Leslie (Hibernian), Sir David Frost and Delia Smith (Norwich City), Liam and Noel Gallagher, Bruce Jones and Kevin Kennedy (Manchester City), James Alexander Gordon (Falkirk), Hugh Grant (Fulham), Alan Green (Macclesfield Town), Nick Hancock (Stoke City), Nigel Havers and Griff Rhys Jones (Ipswich Town), Marie Helvin, Bob Mortimer, Roy "Chubby" Brown and Stephen Tompkinson (Middlesbrough), Tim Henman and Timmy Mallett (Oxford United), John Inverdale (Lincoln City), Lorraine Kelly (Dundee United), John Kettley and Eric Knowles (Burnley), Angus Loughran (Altrincham), Des Lynam, Fat Boy Slim and Jamie Theakston (Brighton & Hove Albion), Robert Lindsay and Tracy Shaw (Derby County), John Major, Suggs and Johnny Vaughan (Chelsea), Peter Mandelson (Hartlepool United), Ewan McGregor (St Johnstone), Bob Mills (Leyton Orient), John Motson (Barnet), Alison Moyet and Terry Alderton (Southend United), Paul Nicholls (Bolton Wanderers), Michael Palin (Sheffield Wednesday), John Parrott (Everton), Alan Parry (Wycombe Wanderers), Jeremy Paxman and Chris Moyles (Leeds United), Robert Plant and Noddy Holder

(Wolverhampton Wanderers), Su Pollard (Nottingham Forest), Vic Reeves (Darlington), Tony Robinson (Bristol City), Carol Smillie and Kirsty Young (Rangers), Patrick Stewart (Huddersfield Town), Tim Vincent (Wrexham), Jo Whiley (Northampton Town), June Whitfield (Wimbledon), Mark Williams (Aston Villa), Robbie Williams (Port Vale) and Catherine Zeta-Jones (Swansea City).

UNITED'S RED ARMY

The following all claim to be ardent Manchester United fans: Mike Atherton, Zoe Ball, Terry Christian, Steve Coogan, Angus Deayton, Eamonn Holmes, Ulrika Jonsson, Mick Hucknall, Morrissey and Gary Rhodes.

VIKING WARRIORS

In the mid-1990s Stenhousemuir (average gate 300) were boosted by the formation of a Norwegian fan club. Each week 100 ardent Scandinavian Stenhousemuir supporters congregated in an Oslo bar to watch videos of the Warriors' games on a large screen. The reason for such long-distance devotion? They liked the name.

OAP AGGRO

Eighty-two-year-old Samuel Phillips was banned by the Herefordshire FA from attending Ledbury Town home games for the rest of the 1980–1 season on account of his unruly behaviour. At the end of the club's home game against Lye, he was alleged to have grabbed the referee by the shirt in protest at the award of a penalty against Ledbury. But the artful pensioner, who had supported Ledbury for nearly 50 years, got round the ban by watching the team through a hedge.

ALTERNATIVE VENUE

Fans of Italian club Padova were in trouble in 1995 after unfurling a banner at the San Paolo Stadium which read: "Stop nuclear tests in Muroroa – do them in Naples instead."

SHOPPING SPREE

In 1994–5 Aberdeen offered fans free coach transport to away games in the hope of encouraging support. But they had to rethink the idea when it emerged that most of the women on board the coaches weren't even going to the match. Instead they were using the free transport to ferry them on shopping expeditions to Glasgow and Edinburgh.

PRESIDENTIAL SUPPORT

Former Soviet President Mikhail Gorbachev once proclaimed himself a keen fan of Wigan Athletic! His interest stemmed from the time when he was a member of the entourage of Russian team Metallist Khartrov when they came over to play a friendly at Wigan in the 1969–70 season.

CRITIC BANNED

Forty-two-year-old Terry Jamieson, a governor at Albany Prison on the Isle of Wight, was banned from watching his local team, Newport FC, in 1991 for persistent heckling from the touchline. The club told him his comments "transcended the acceptable". His criticism of the team followed seven home games in which Newport had failed to score.

FANS' FAVOURITE

Coventry City fans were incensed by manager Jimmy Hill's decision to sell folk hero George Hudson to Northampton in March 1966 on the eve of City's FA Cup fifth round tie with Everton. So hundreds of them travelled to watch Hudson at Northampton rather than go to Merseyside to witness a "Hudsonless" Sky Blues. They were shrewd judges. Coventry lost 3–0.

IRON WORKERS FIRED

The chairman of Cannon Iron Foundries, Staffordshire, announced in January 1952 that 11 iron moulders who took time off to see Wolves play Manchester City in a third round FA Cup replay would be dismissed. Their action had meant that 24 others had to stop work and they too had gone to the match.

VEGGIE VANDAL

A Bolton fan was fined £60 and banned from the ground for three months in 1995 after admitting throwing a turnip in front of Wolves manager Graham Taylor.

INJURED BY OWN FAN

Plymouth striker Dwight Marshall was injured by one of his own fans after scoring at Chester in 1999. As Marshall saluted the goal, the fan ran on to the pitch to join in the celebration but his over-exuberance left the player nursing an injured leg. The travelling fans had no further cause for celebration as Chester went on to win 3–2.

BOROUGH'S BEST FRIEND

In 1998 Scarborough awarded club membership to one of their most loyal fans – an eight-year-old lurcher dog called Honey.

PRAM PUSHER

Forty-eight-year-old Swiss soccer fan Emil Holliger, a window-cleaner by trade, announced in June 1966 that he intended to push a pram, decked with national colours and cowbells, across Europe to Sheffield where, on 12 July, the Swiss met West Germany in their opening tie in the World Cup finals.

THE THREE LITTLE PIGS

In November 1998, Wolfie, mascot of Wolverhampton Wanderers, was involved in a half-time punch-up with three little pigs at Bristol City's Ashton Gate ground. The pigs were hosting a children's penalty shoot-out to promote a double-glazing firm but tempers became frayed between the animals, one of which was seen to aim a trotter at Wolfie. The Bristol City mascot, City Cat, tried to intervene but the bad feeling continued near the tunnel as the animals trooped off. Eventually, they had to be separated by stewards. One of the pigs later accused Wolfie of giving him a cut lip. A spokesman for Avon and Somerset police said: "We were not involved but we understand there was a lot of huffing and puffing."

14

THE AGE GAP

OLD BILL

The oldest player to turn out in an FA Cup tie was Billy Meredith of Manchester City. He was 49 years, eight months old when he played in the 1924 semi-final against Newcastle.

CRISIS MANAGEMENT

The oldest player to appear in a Football League match was New Brighton manager Neil McBain who stepped in as emergency goalkeeper at Hartlepool United in a Third Division (North) fixture on 15 March 1947 at the age of 51 years, 120 days.

CUP YOUNGSTERS

Paul Allen became the youngest man to appear in a Wembley FA Cup Final in the twentieth century when he played for West Ham in 1980 at the age of 17 years, 256 days. But he was positively ancient compared to Worcester City's Andy Awford who was just 15 years and 88 days old when he featured in a third qualifying round tie against Boreham Wood in 1987.

FRESH OUT OF NAPPIES

Sunderland's Derek Forster earned the distinction of becoming the youngest player to appear in the First Division when he kept goal against Leicester City on 22 August 1964. He was 15 years, 185 days. But two players made their Football League bow when they were 27 days younger. On 16 September 1929 Albert Geldard appeared for Bradford Park Avenue against Millwall, aged 15 years, 158 days. And Ken Roberts was precisely the same age when he made his debut for Wrexham against Bradford Park Avenue on 1 September 1951. However, these three were positive veterans compared to Eamonn Collins of Blackpool. He was a mere 14 years, 322 days when he came on as substitute in an Anglo-Scottish Cup tie with Kilmarnock on 9 September 1980.

YOUNG TON

Chelsea's Jimmy Greaves is the youngest player to have scored 100 Football League goals. He reached that milestone against Manchester City on 19 November 1960, aged 20 years, 261 days.

JASON'S JOY

The youngest player to score in the top flight of the Football League was schoolboy Jason Dozzell who came on as substitute for Ipswich Town against Coventry on 4 February 1984 at the age of 16 years, 57 days. He went on to score Ipswich's third goal in a 3–1 win.

LATE DEVELOPER

The oldest player to win his first England cap was Leslie Compton. He was 38 years, 2 months when he made his international bow against Wales on 15 November 1950.

COVER BLOWN

Before Paul Allen, the distinction of being the youngest player to appear in an FA Cup Final had fallen to Howard Kendall. He was 17 years, 345 days old when he took the field for Preston against West Ham in the 1964 final. Yet Kendall only forced his way into the team after first choice Ian Davidson was suspended by the club for pretending to be at a funeral when he should have been playing in a League game.

ROGER AND OUT

Forty-two-year-old Roger Milla became the oldest player to score in the World Cup when he netted

Cameroon's consolation in their 6–1 drubbing by Russia at the 1994 tournament.

DUNCAN'S DEBUT

When Duncan Edwards ran on to the Old Trafford pitch on Easter Monday 1953 for the First Division fixture with Cardiff City, he was aged 16 years, 185 days and was the youngest player ever to turn out for United. Sadly for Edwards, Cardiff spoiled his day by winning 4–1.

YOUNG IMP

Appointed manager of Lincoln City in 1972 at the age of 28, Graham Taylor became the youngest-ever manager in the history of the Football League.

NORMAN'S CONQUESTS

Norman Whiteside of Manchester United and Northern Ireland holds two age records. His goal against Liverpool in the 1983 League Cup Final made Whiteside (at 17 years, 324 days) the youngest goalscorer in a Wembley Cup Final. And a few months later, his goal against Brighton in the 1983 replay made him the youngest FA Cup Final goalscorer. He was 18 years, 19 days.

YOUNG AND OLD

The youngest player to be capped by England was James Prinsep who was 17 years, 252 days when playing against Scotland on 5 April 1879. The youngest England scorer was Michael Owen who was 18 years, 164 days when he found the net against Morocco on 27 May 1998. The oldest player to be capped by England was Stanley Matthews who played his final international against Denmark, on 15 May 1957, aged 42 years, 104 days. Age was no bar to Matthews. On 6 February 1965 he turned out for Stoke City in a First Division match with Fulham when he was five days past his 50th birthday.

GOING FOR EXPERIENCE

When Bradford City made the trip to Leicester for a crucial Premiership match on 6 May 2000, three Bradford players – John Dreyer, Stuart McCall and Dean Saunders – were older than the club's manager, Paul Jewell.

15

FANTASTIC FEATS

SHEARER CLASS

With 31 goals in 1993–4, 34 in 1994–5 and 31 in
1995–6, Alan Shearer became the first player to score
over 30 top-flight goals in three successive seasons
since the war.

ALL CONQUERING

Celtic won no fewer than five major trophies in 1966–7 –
the European Cup, the Scottish League, the Scottish FA
Cup, the Scottish League Cup and the Glasgow Cup.

ENTERTAINING CITY

Manchester City became the first club to score and
concede 100 Football League goals in a season when

they scored 104 and let in 100 in season 1957–8. Despite giving away more than two goals a game, they still managed to finish fifth in Division One. But City's capacity to entertain had proved their downfall 20 years previously. For they finished 1937–8 as the highest-scoring team in the First Division with 80 goals. But their leaky defence (77 goals conceded) meant that they finished 21st and were relegated.

FORTRESS SPOTLAND

Rochdale didn't concede a home goal in Division Three (North) in season 1923–4 until 15 December when they let in a penalty against Barrow.

SUMMERS' DAY

In what was arguably the most remarkable comeback of all time, Charlton Athletic beat Huddersfield Town 7–6 at The Valley on 21 December 1957 after trailing 1–5 with just 38 minutes to go. The hero of the half-hour was Johnny Summers with five goals despite the fact that he was wearing new boots which hadn't even been broken in.

RUNAWAY CHAMPIONS

Winning the Scottish League Championship in 1958,

Hearts scored 132 goals and conceded just 29, giving them a record goal difference of plus 103.

WEBB'S WONDER

With both regular goalkeepers unfit, Chelsea were forced to play defender David Webb between the posts for the entire match against Ipswich on 27 December 1971. What's more, Webb kept a clean sheet, his safe hands guiding Chelsea to a 2–0 win.

UNITED SUPREME

Manchester United won four of the first five Carling Premiership titles. And in the year they missed out – 1995 – they still finished second. Their League and FA Cup success of 1998–9 made them the first club to do the double on three occasions.

DROUGHT ENDED

When Cardiff won at Orient on 1 December 1973, it was the Bluebirds' first away win for over two years.

GUNNERS FIRE BLANKS

Arsenal's 5–0 beating at the hands of Chelsea in a 1998

Worthington Cup tie was the club's heaviest defeat for 73 years.

TIGHT DEFENCE

In the 1978–9 League season, Liverpool conceded just four goals at home and only 16 goals in 42 First Division games. This defensive record enabled them to win the title by eight points. Manchester United also conceded only four goals at home in 1994–5.

A MIXED MONTH

Bristol City defender David Rodgers scored in four successive Division One matches in 1978 – twice for City and twice for the opposition. On 26 August he scored the only goal of the game against visiting Aston Villa but undid all the good work the following week by putting through his own goal as Wolves won 2–0. On 9 September another Rodgers own goal sent City sliding to defeat at Tottenham but he redeemed himself the following Saturday with a goal at the right end as City beat Southampton 3–1.

FIRST WIN IN LONDON

When Rochdale won 4–0 at Barnet in 1995, it was the club's first ever victory in London.

CLEAN SWEEP

In season 1929–30, Rangers won every competition they entered – the Scottish League, the Scottish FA Cup, the Reserve Cup, the Reserve Championship, the Glasgow Cup and the Glasgow Charity Cup.

WHAT GOES UP ...

Northampton Town became the first club to rise from the Fourth Division to the First when they climbed through the divisions in just five seasons between 1961 and 1965. Unfortunately their demise was just as swift and, after just one season in the top flight, by 1969 they were back in the Fourth Division. Watford also climbed from Fourth to First in five seasons between 1978 and 1982, while Swansea City went one better with three promotions in four seasons (1978–1981).

SEVENTH HEAVEN

In 1998 Birmingham City pulled off two 7–0 away wins in the First Division. On 10 January they won 7–0 at Stoke and on 12 December they produced the same scoreline at Oxford.

GRAND ACHIEVEMENT

On 23 January 1999, Stenhousemuir defender Graeme

Armstrong played his 1000th senior game when he turned out in a Scottish FA Cup tie against Rangers at Ibrox. He was presented with the Man of the Match award before kick-off! Armstrong's career had begun 24 years earlier as a one-match trialist with Meadowbank Thistle. He went on to play for Stirling Albion, Berwick Rangers, Meadowbank and, from 1992, Stenhousemuir.

IN A LEAGUE OF THEIR OWN

Coventry City are the only club to have played in the Premiership, all four divisions in the previous structure of the Football League, plus both sections of the old Third Division (North and South).

SHOCK DEFEAT

Newcastle United won the First Division Championship in 1908–9 despite crashing 9–1 at home to neighbours Sunderland on 5 December, eight of the Sunderland goals coming in a 28-minute spell in the second half. This stood as the biggest away win in the First Division until it was equalled by Wolves at Cardiff on 3 September 1955.

CREWE ON A ROLL

Crewe Alexandra won 16 home games on the trot in 1938 – the last ten in one season and the first six of the next.

GEORGIE'S TRAVELS

In the space of ten days in 1977, George Best played in all four British countries. He played for Northern Ireland in Belfast and for Fulham at home to Crystal Palace, away to Cardiff and in a friendly at St Mirren.

MILAN MARVELS

On 21 March 1993, Parma ended Milan's 58-match unbeaten run in the Italian League.

DEFENCE BREACHED

When Manchester United suffered a shock 2–1 home defeat to Nottingham Forest on 17 December 1994, they were the first League goals United had conceded at Old Trafford for 1135 minutes (over 12 matches).

DUNDEE CAKEWALK

Dundee powered to a club record 10–0 victory over Alloa Athletic in a Second Division match on 9 March 1947. To prove it was no fluke, they repeated the feat 13 days later against Dunfermline.

SCORED TWO AT BOTH ENDS

Two players in Football League history have managed to score two goals for both sides in a match. Sam Wynne of Oldham Athletic scored all four goals in his side's 2–2 draw with Manchester United in a Second Division game on 6 October 1923. And Aston Villa's Chris Nicholl also managed to score two own goals and two at the right end, in a First Division game against Leicester City on 20 March 1976.

NINE IN A ROW

Rangers and Celtic have both won the Scottish League title in nine successive years. Celtic's reign lasted from 1966 until 1974 under Jock Stein while Rangers were invincible between 1989 and 1997.

GREAT COMEBACKS

On 9 March 1996, Ipswich Town were 0–3 down at Barnsley with five minutes left, but fought back to snatch a 3–3 draw. Trailing 4–0 at half-time, Queens Park Rangers were still 1–4 down at Port Vale with five minutes left of their First Division encounter on 19 January 1997. But they scored three late goals to claim an improbable 4–4 draw. On 12 April 1993, Swindon Town were 1–4 down at Birmingham City with half an hour to play, but stormed back to win 6–4. And back on 12 November 1904, Sheffield Wednesday raced into a 5–0 lead at half-time against Everton, only

for the visitors to score five second-half goals and earn a
5–5 draw.

NON-SCORERS

Defender Ray Wilcox played 489 League games for
Newport County between 1946 and 1959 without
once scoring. Blackpool and Manchester City centre-
half Roy Gratrix also failed to score in his 415-League
game career from 1953 to 1964. Richard Robinson, a
full-back with Middlesbrough and Barrow, bagged just
one goal in 525 League outings between 1946 and
1962.

THE RISE OF THE DONS

By finishing third in Division Two in 1986, Wimbledon
had risen from non-League football to the First Division
in a mere nine years. And in 1988 they won the FA Cup.

PALACE BREAK LONDON HOODOO

Crystal Palace's 2–0 victory over Chelsea on 31 March
1973 was their first over a London club in 32 attempts
since their promotion to the First Division in 1969. Not
that it did Palace much good – they were relegated at
the end of the season.

CLARETS' UNBEATEN RUN

After losing their opening three matches of the 1920–1 season, Burnley tasted defeat in only three of their remaining 39 games to lift the Football League Championship for the first time in their history. Sunderland were another Championship-winning side to make a dodgy start. They took only two points from their opening seven matches in 1912–13 but won 25 of the remaining 31 games to clinch their fifth League title.

FOREST CUT DOWN

Millwall's 2–0 victory at Nottingham Forest on 30 November 1994 made them the first team to win a League Cup tie at the City Ground for 18 years.

DISMAL RECORDS

Rochdale won just two matches out of 46 when finishing bottom of the Third Division in season 1973–4, an echo of their 1931–2 season in Third Division (North) when they picked up a mere 11 points, having lost 33 games out of 40. Stoke City lost 31 games out of 42 and finished 23 points adrift of second-bottom Sunderland when they were relegated from the First Division in 1985. In Scotland, Forfar Athletic won just one Second Division match out of 38 in 1974–5 and Clydebank managed just one victory out of 36 in 1999–2000. By a strange coincidence, Forfar and Clydebank recorded their only successes against the same team . . . Raith Rovers.

SAVAGED BY WOLVES

Trailing 1–5 after the first leg of the 1958 FA Youth Cup Final, Wolves powered back to beat Chelsea 6–1 in the second leg and snatch the trophy 7–6 on aggregate.

IPSWICH BREAK THEIR DUCK

When Ipswich Town won 1–0 at Liverpool on 14 January 1995, it was their first victory at Anfield in 28 attempts.

LONG THROW

Tranmere Rovers' defender Dave Challinor boasts the longest throw of any footballer in the world – over 50 yards.

SWINDON SWAMPED

In 1994 Swindon Town became the first team in the top division to concede 100 League goals in a season since Ipswich 30 years earlier.

AUSTIN'S POWERS

Terry Austin played a record 49 Football League games in season 1978–9 – 33 for Walsall and 16 for Mansfield Town.

TEL STAR

Terry Venables is the only player to have represented England at schoolboy, youth, amateur, under-23 and full international level.

MULTI-CHAMPIONS

Wolves and Burnley are the only clubs to have won the championships of the old Divisions One, Two, Three and Four. Wolves were also champions of Third Division (North).

SPIREITES' GOLDEN YEAR

Chesterfield scored in 46 consecutive Third Division (North) games between Christmas Day 1929 and Boxing Day 1930 – a Football League record.

THE LESS THAN ADMIRABLE NELSON

Nelson once lost 24 away games in a row in Third Division (North). They lost the last three of the

1929–30 season and then all 21 the following term.
After that, they dropped out of the Football League.

CLAIM TO FAME

Although Celtic have won the Scottish FA Cup on 30
occasions – more than any other club – they have never
lifted the trophy three years in succession. That honour
rests with Queen's Park (1874–6 and 1880–2), Rangers
(1934–6, 1948–50 and 1962–4) and Aberdeen (1982–4).

READY AND ABEL

Atletico Madrid goalkeeper Abel Resino set a new world
record by going 1275 minutes without conceding a goal
in 1990–1 season. He was finally beaten by Sporting
Gijon's Enrique on 19 March 1991. Even so, Atletico
still won 3–1.

AWAY-DAY SPECIALISTS

On their away to winning the Division Three (North)
title in 1946–7, Doncaster Rovers won 18 of their 21
away games. Of their two defeats, one was against
bottom-of-the-table Halifax Town.

SMALL IS BEST

Liverpool and Aston Villa each used only 14 players

when they won the League Championship in 1965–6 and 1980–1 respectively. At the other end of the scale, Birmingham City under Barry Fry used no fewer than 46 players during an unsuccessful 1995–6 season.

VALE ON THE UP

Port Vale prevented the opposition from scoring in 30 of their 46 games on the way to winning the Division Three (North) title by 11 points in 1953–4.

UNBEATEN FOR 25 ROUNDS

Liverpool went unbeaten for 25 rounds of the Football League Cup. Following a semi-final defeat by Nottingham Forest in 1980, Liverpool remained undefeated in the competition until Tottenham toppled them in a third-round tie on 31 October 1984. During that period, the men from Anfield won the League Cup four times.

COURAGEOUS COUNTY

With three of their players stuck in snow en route to a Fourth Division game at Bury in April 1981, Stockport County had to play the entire first half with only nine men. Even so, they managed to battle to a 1–0 win.

STARS OF THE FUTURE

Manchester United won the FA Youth Cup for the first five years of its existence, between 1953 and 1957. In the 1956 final they beat Chesterfield 4–3. One of United's scorers was a young Bobby Charlton while in goal for Chesterfield that day was Gordon Banks. Ten years later, they played together in England's victorious World Cup team.

KILLIE KILLJOYS

Celtic went a record 62 Scottish League games unbeaten between 13 November 1915 and 21 April 1917, when Kilmarnock won 2–0 at Parkhead.

MERTHYR, SHE WROTE

The name of Merthyr Town was written into the record books when they went 61 away League games without a win between 1922 and 1925 in Third Division (South).

FOUR FOR DELANEY

Jimmy Delaney won FA Cup medals in four different countries. He was a member of the Celtic side which won the Scottish FA Cup in 1937; he played for

Manchester United when they won the FA Cup in 1948; he was with Irish Cup winners Derry City in 1954; and in 1956 he picked up a losers' medal when Cork Athletic were beaten by Shamrock Rovers in the final of the FA of Ireland Cup.

UNCHANGED DEFENCE

The entire six-man defence of Huddersfield Town were ever-present for the 42 matches in Division Two in season 1952–3.

BARREN SPELLS

Hartlepool went two months without scoring in 1993. Over a period of 13 games and 1221 minutes, they failed to score in 11 Second Division matches, one FA Cup tie and an Autoglass Shield Trophy tie. The spell was finally broken on 6 March at Blackpool by Andy Saville. Crystal Palace set a Premiership record when they went nine matches in a row without scoring in 1994–5.

STIRLING WORK

Stirling Albion hold the British senior record for the longest scoreless run. They went 14 matches and 1292 minutes in 1981 without finding the net. Yet three years later they were hammering Selkirk 20–0 in a first round Scottish Cup tie, the biggest victory in British senior football since 1891. Stirling were 15–0 up at half-time and no fewer than nine of their players found their way on to the scoresheet.

CLEAN SHEETS

Rangers' Chris Woods holds the British goalkeeping record for the longest shut-out by not conceding a goal for 1196 minutes in 1986–7. He was finally beaten by a strike from Adrian Sprott of Hamilton Academicals, which, sensationally, turned out to be the only goal of a third round Scottish FA Cup tie. In 1995–6, Gillingham keeper Jim Stannard set a new Football League record by keeping 29 clean sheets in 46 matches.

HELPING HAND

After injuring a hand during the match with Halifax in 1962, Reading keeper Arthur Wilkie came out of goal and played as a forward. He went on to score twice in Reading's 4–2 win.

MEDAL MOUNTAIN

Trevor Steven won League Championship medals in three different countries. He won two titles in England with Everton (1985 and 1987), five in Scotland with Rangers (1990, 1991, 1993, 1994 and 1995) and in between, one in France with Marseille (1992).

INVINCIBLE CELTS

Celtic remained unbeaten in Scottish League football for nearly 18 months between November 1915 and April 1917 – a total of 62 matches.

MANSFIELD BITTER

In 1971–2, Mansfield Town failed to score in any of their first nine home games in Division Three. They were relegated at the end of the season.

UNBEATEN

Two Football League teams have managed to go through the entire season unbeaten – Preston North End in 1888–9 (22 matches) and Liverpool in the Second Division in 1893–4 (28 matches). The closest to repeating that achievement in modern times was in 1990–1 when Arsenal lost just one out of 38 matches on their way to becoming First Division champions.

UNBEATEN FOR MORE THAN A YEAR

Nottingham Forest hold the record for the longest

unbeaten run in the Football League – 42 matches (21 wins and 21 draws) between November 1977 and December 1978. Their run finally came to an end at Liverpool.

FLYING STARTS

Leeds in 1973–4 and Liverpool in 1987–8 both went unbeaten for 29 League matches at the start of the First Division season. Liverpool had won 22 and drawn seven before going down to Everton, of all clubs. Everton's winning goal came from Wayne Clarke whose older brother, Allan, was a member of the 1973–4 Leeds team.

UNIQUE TREBLE

Bobby Moore and Geoff Hurst collected a hat-trick of winners' medals in the Sixties, in three different competitions at Wembley. In 1964 they were in the West Ham side that won the FA Cup; the following year they were members of the Hammers' victorious European Cup Winners' Cup team; and, of course, in 1966 they were key players in England's World Cup triumph.

EARLY CELEBRATIONS

So dominant were Morton in 1963–4 season that they clinched the Scottish Second Division title as early as 29 February. They won their first 23 matches, finished with 135 goals from their 36 League games and dropped just five points all season.

TOP MARK

Chesterfield goalkeeper Mark Leonard kept a clean sheet for eight consecutive away games in Division Three in 1994.

ELLAND ROAD GLOOM

After winning the League Championship in 1992, Leeds United went through the whole of the following season without recording an away win in the League – a unique achievement.

STRAIGHT DEFEATS

Darwen lost a record 18 Football League games in a row in 1898–9. Walsall nearly matched them in 1988–9 when they lost 15 Second Division games on the trot. And Manchester United suffered an appalling start to the 1930–1 season, losing their first 12 games in Division One.

MISERABLE START

Newport County went a record 25 League matches without a win in Division Four at the start of the

281

1970–1 season, managing just four draws over that period. They finally broke the spell on 15 January with a 3–0 victory over Southend United.

QUEEN'S REIGN SUPREME

Queen's Park did not concede a single goal in the first seven years of their existence between 1867 and 1874.

RINGING THE CHANGES

In April 1986 West Ham centre-half Alvin Martin scored a hat-trick against three different goalkeepers in the Hammers' 8–1 trouncing of Newcastle. Martin Thomas was replaced in the Newcastle goal first by Chris Hedworth and then by Peter Beardsley.

DRAW SPECIALISTS

In 1997–8, Cardiff City and Hartlepool United both drew half of their 46 matches in Division Three. But Norwich City had an even higher percentage of drawn games in the First Division in 1978–9. They also had 23 draws, but from only 42 matches.

HOME BANKERS

Sunderland lost only once in 73 home games in Division One between 1891 and 1896.

GLUT OF DRAWS

On 18 September 1948, nine of the 11 matches in the First Division of the Football League finished as draws.

ANFIELD UNTAMED

Liverpool went 85 competitive matches unbeaten at Anfield between 21 January 1978 and 31 January 1981 (when they lost 2–1 to Leicester City). The run covered 63 League games, nine League Cup, seven in Europe and six in the FA Cup. Ironically, Leicester were relegated that season.

PRIDE OF LIONS

Millwall remained unbeaten at home in the Football League for 59 matches in a row between 1964 and 1967 before the run was eventually broken by Plymouth Argyle. What made the Lions' achievement all the more laudable was that they had to adjust to life in different divisions since their unbeaten run saw them rise from the Fourth to the Second.

CANTONA'S TREBLE

Eric Cantona won three different League Championships with different teams in successive seasons. In 1990–1 he won the French First Division with Marseille; in 1991–2 he lifted the English First Division with

Leeds United; and in 1992–3 he won the newly created Premiership with Manchester United.

THE GOOD AND THE BAD

Nottingham Forest hold the record for the best and worst runs in the Premiership. Between February and November 1995, they went 25 League games unbeaten until they were mauled 7–0 at Blackburn. But in season 1998–9 they went 19 League games without a win en route to relegation to the Nationwide League.

CAMBRIDGE IN FREEFALL

The longest sequence without a victory in the Football League was set by Cambridge United in 1983–4. They went 31 matches without a win in the Second Division between 8 October and 23 April, losing 21 of them. Not surprisingly, they finished at the foot of the table. They didn't fare any better the following year in Division Three, again winning just four games all season and finishing bottom of the table.

EIGHT YEARS UNBEATEN

Real Madrid went eight years unbeaten at home in the Spanish League. After losing to neighbours Atletico Madrid on 3 February 1957, Real played 122 home games without defeat until they were finally beaten on 7 March 1965 . . . again by Atletico.

MERSEY MARVELS

Liverpool is the only English city to have staged top-flight football in every season since the Football League started in 1888.

SHILTON'S LANDMARK

Goalkeeper Peter Shilton became the first man to appear in 1000 Football League games when he played for Leyton Orient against Brighton & Hove Albion in December 1996. In true Shilton tradition, he kept a clean sheet.

MODEL T FORD

On 16 January 1999, Mansfield winger and consummate professional Tony Ford made his 825th League appearance (a record for an outfield player) in the Third Division fixture at Plymouth. Ford's total surpassed that of former Southampton and England wide man Terry Paine.

ONE-CLUB MAN

Full-back John Trollope holds the record for the most

appearances with one Football League club – 770 for Swindon Town between 1960 and 1980.

KING HAROLD

Tranmere Rovers' centre-half Harold Bell made a record 459 consecutive appearances for the club between 1946 and 1955.

HOME SWEET HOME

Only two Football League teams have won all their home games in a season. Liverpool won all 14 in Division Two in 1893–4 and Brentford won all 21 matches at Griffin Park in Division Three (South) in 1929–30. Rotherham United almost equalled Brentford's feat in 1946–7 but after 20 straight wins at Millmoor, they could only draw their final Third Division (North) fixture.

16

SIGNING ON

SWAPPED FOR PORK

In 1998, midfielder Ion Radu was sold by Romanian Second Division club Jiul Petrosani to Valcea for 500 kilos of pork, worth about £1750.

MILLION-POUND MAN

Trevor Francis became Britain's first million-pound footballer when he was transferred from Birmingham City to Nottingham Forest in 1979. No sooner had he broken the transfer record than Forest manager Brian Clough consigned Francis to the third team.

CAR EXCHANGE

In 1981 it was reported that Spanish footballer Juan

Lozano, who had signed a three-year contract with Anderlecht, would become a Belgian citizen in exchange for a Porsche sports car.

COSTLY COMMON

The first £1000 player was Alf Common who was transferred from Sunderland to Middlesbrough in 1905.

LAW BREAKER

Denis Law became the first British £100,000 player when he was transferred from Manchester City to Italian club Torino in the summer of 1961. A year later he broke the British transfer record for a second time when he returned to Manchester – this time United – for £115,000.

POPE WAS BLESSED

On 7 February 1925, Albert Pope travelled to Old Trafford as a member of the Clapton Orient team for a Second Division game with Manchester United. But before the kick-off he signed for United and the transfer was cleared by phone so that he could play in the match for the Reds. To round off a memorable day, he scored United's fourth goal in a 4–2 victory.

THE FEE WAS DICTATED

When Romanian midfield star Georghe Hagi moved from Sportul Studentesc to Steaua Bucharest in 1986, it was on a free transfer despite the fact that Hagi was already an established international and the League's top scorer. The controversial lack of fee may have had something to do with the fact that Romania's ruling Ceaucescu family just happened to be directors of Steaua . . .

BALL BREAKER

The first player to be transferred for £100,000 between two English clubs was Alan Ball when he moved from Blackpool to Everton for £110,000 in 1966. Two years later Colin Stein became the first player to move for a six-figure fee between two Scottish clubs when Hibernian sold him to Rangers.

A LOAD OF BALLS

Middlesbrough signed Gary Pallister from Billingham Synthonia for a bag of balls and a set of shirts. Another future international who cost only a set of shirts was Republic of Ireland striker Tony Cascarino when he signed for Gillingham from Kent amateur club Crockenhill.

A POUND SHORT

When Jimmy Greaves ended his six-month stint in Italy with AC Milan by signing for Spurs in December 1961, manager Bill Nicholson set the transfer fee at £99,999 because he didn't want Greaves to be burdened with the tag of being Britain's first £100,000 footballer.

MORE HASTE . . .

Eager to beat off the other 26 clubs who were keen to sign Scottish schoolboy sensation Peter Lorimer, Leeds United boss Don Revie was in such a hurry to obtain Lorimer's signature that he was stopped for speeding on the way to his house.

MILLION-POUND KEEPER

Bristol Rovers' Nigel Martyn became Britain's first million-pound goalkeeper when he signed for Crystal Palace in 1989.

MILES APART

The biggest discrepancy in a transfer which went to a tribunal occurred in June 1994 with the sale of striker Andy Walker from Bolton Wanderers to Celtic. Bolton wanted £2.2 million, but Celtic offered only £250,000. The tribunal fixed the fee at £550,000.

GOAL IN A MILLION

David Platt scored just three goals in 16 League games for Juventus after joining the Turin club for £6.5 million in 1992. Although Juve managed to recoup a fair proportion of the money when they sold Platt on to Sampdoria, his goals still cost them in the region of £1 million each.

WHO'S THE BOSS?

Julian Broddle found himself playing under no fewer than six different managers during a three-month period in 1989–90 season. While Broddle was at Barnsley, Allan Clarke was sacked and Eric Winstanley took over as caretaker manager until Mel Machin took permanent charge. In January Machin sold Broddle to Plymouth but no sooner had he arrived at Home Park than the Devon club's manager Ken Brown was axed. John Gregory was appointed caretaker until David Kemp took over in February.

BARGAN BUY

Romanian Fourth Division club Recolta Laza lost goalkeeper Valentin Bargan in 1998 when he was lured away to Stemnic Buda by an offer of £8 and a load of firewood.

MAC THE KNIFE

Shortly after signing flamboyant striker Duncan McKenzie for Leeds United in 1974, Brian Clough was sacked as manager. Three years later, McKenzie was sold to Everton. Introducing his new signing to the press, manager Billy Bingham joked: "The last time a manager signed him, he got the sack a couple of weeks later!" Sure enough, within a few weeks Bingham too got the sack.

COULDN'T SETTLE

Less than a week after joining Aston Villa from West Ham in 1998, defender David Unsworth returned to his first club, Everton. Apparently his wife hadn't wanted to move to Birmingham.

ALLEN'S MILLIONS

Clive Allen was the first British player to be the subject of three £1 million transfer deals. In June 1980 he became Britain's first £1 million teenager when, at 19, he moved from Queens Park Rangers to Arsenal. Two months later, Arsenal recouped their money when they sold him to Crystal Palace. And in 1988, Spurs sold Allen to French club Bordeaux for another cool million.

IT ALL CAME OUT IN THE WASH

When future Scottish international Jim Baxter signed

for Fife junior side Crossgates Primrose from Halbeath Boys' Club, he officially cost Crossgates a fee of £2 10s. But it later emerged that they had also slipped him an extra £30 so that his mum could buy a washing machine.

SNATCH OF THE DAY

After being beaten by bitter rivals Moscow Dynamo in 1947, Kiev coveted the three star players of Odessa Pishchevik. Rather than pay a conventional transfer fee, Kiev had the trio kidnapped in broad daylight.

17

INTO EUROPE

REAL TRIUMPH

Real Madrid won the 2000 UEFA Champions' League despite losing three times to Bayern Munich en route to the final. Real lost twice to the Germans in group matches and were also beaten by them in the second leg of the semi-final. However, the Spanish team went through on aggregate.

LATIN DOMINANCE

Real Madrid won the first five European Champions' Cup Finals, from 1956 to 1960. Their dominance was finally ended by arch rivals Barcelona in 1961 although Barca themselves were beaten in the final by Benfica of Portugal. It was not until Celtic's triumph in 1967 that a non-Latin club lifted the European Cup.

ENGLISH SUPREMACY

English clubs lifted the European Champions' Cup for a record six consecutive years between 1977 and 1982. Liverpool won in 1977 and 1978, Nottingham Forest took over for the next two years, Liverpool won again in 1981 and Aston Villa triumphed in 1982.

BLUE IS THE COLOUR

Chelsea showed no sympathy to Luxembourg part-timers Jeunesse Hautcharage in a first round tie in the 1971–2 European Cup Winners' Cup. Chelsea won 21–0 over the two legs.

WRIGHT ON

Ian Wright became the first player to score in each leg of every round for a club reaching a European final. He did it playing for Arsenal in the 1994–5 European Cup Winners' Cup. But then he failed to score in the final itself, which Arsenal lost to Real Zaragoza, courtesy of Nayim's 45-yard lob over David Seaman in the last minute of extra time.

STUCK IN TRAFFIC

Trailing 4–1 to Standard Liege after a disastrous first leg in Belgium, Rangers needed all the help they could get for their 1962 European Cup quarter-final at Ibrox. But they had to make do without influential winger Willie

Henderson who arrived too late to play after being held up in traffic. In his absence, Rangers went out 4–3 on aggregate.

BERGKAMP GROUNDED

Arsenal's Dutch ace Dennis Bergkamp refuses to play in any European tie if it necessitates flying. He will only go if he can reach the ground in question by road or rail.

TOO LITTLE, TOO LATE

Manchester United keeper Peter Schmeichel headed an 89th-minute equaliser from Ryan Giggs' corner to earn a 2–2 draw with Rotor Volgograd of Russia in a UEFA Cup tie in 1995. But United went out of the competition on away goals.

GOAL MACHINE

Alfredo di Stefano of Real Madrid scored an incredible 49 goals in 58 European Cup matches, including a hat-trick in the 1960 final against Eintracht Frankfurt, which Real won 7–3.

SPINK THE HERO

When Aston Villa met Bayern Munich in the final of the 1982 European Cup, their plans were hit by an injury to goalkeeper Jimmy Rimmer who had to go off after just eight minutes. His place was taken by 23-year-old Nigel Spink, a reserve keeper with only one first-team appearance to his name. But Spink rose to the occasion and kept a clean sheet as Villa won 1–0 thanks to a goal from Peter Withe.

MISSED OUT

As a result of the ban imposed on English clubs in Europe following the Heysel disaster of 1985, four English clubs who had never previously played in a European competition were denied their chance – Norwich City, Oxford United, Luton Town and Wimbledon.

EUROPEAN TRAILBLAZERS

Birmingham City were the first English club to reach the final of a European competition. In 1960 they got to the final of the Inter Cities Fairs Cup (the forerunner to the UEFA Cup), only to lose 4–1 over two legs to Barcelona. They did it again in 1961, this time losing in the final to Roma.

BALL OF CONFUSION

Rangers won the European Cup Winners' Cup in 1972 despite losing a penalty shoot-out against Sporting Lisbon in the second round. The Scots had won the tie on away goals but the referee was confused about the rules and ordered a penalty competition which Sporting won. The decision was subsequently revoked, allowing Rangers through to the next round.

FIVE OUT OF SIX

Between 1989 and 1995, the UEFA Cup was won by an Italian club five times out of six. The only Italian side to miss out were Torino in 1992, beaten by Ajax on the away goal rule after drawing 2–2 on aggregate.

COKE-HEAD

Trailing 2–4 from the first leg, Borussia Moenchengladbach hammered Inter Milan 7–1 in a second round European Champions' Cup tie in 1971–2 to win 9–5 on aggregate. But during the second game one of the Inter players was hit on the head by a Coca-Cola bottle thrown from the crowd and the Italians appealed successfully against the result. A replay was ordered and this time Inter held the Germans to a 0–0 draw, a score which enabled them to progress to the next round and ultimately go all the way to the final.

FOWLER FALLS FOUL

Robbie Fowler fell foul of UEFA after lifting his shirt to reveal a vest pledging support for the striking Liverpool dockers during a European Cup Winners' Cup match with Brann of Norway. Fowler was fined £900.

RUSSIAN RAGE

Glasgow Rangers manager Graeme Souness sparked a diplomatic row in 1987 when he decided to reduce the width of the Ibrox pitch before the second leg of a European Cup first round tie with Dynamo Kiev. The aim was to counter the threat of the visiting wingmen, but the Russians protested and accused Rangers of unsportsmanlike behaviour. "There used to be gentlemen in British football," raged Kiev secretary Mikhail Oshenkov. "That is clearly not the case at Glasgow Rangers." However, Rangers' 2–0 win (which gave them a 2–1 aggregate victory) was allowed to stand when UEFA declared the pitch to be 20cm inside the minimum requirements.

18

FOR CLUB AND COUNTRY

TOOK DEFEAT BADLY

After Algeria had been eliminated from the qualifying rounds for the 1998 World Cup by Kenya, the Algerian king and his government banned the national coach and his deputy from working in football for life and also dissolved the National League.

SAW RED

Irate Chinese players marched round the pitch at Bogota before a friendly with Colombia in 1978 waving their country's red flag. The protest was aimed at the Colombian Police Band who had mistakenly played the Taiwanese national anthem instead of the Chinese. The impromptu march delayed the kick-off for half an hour.

CAPTAIN SHOT

The first captain to lead out a team in a World Cup match was later shot on suspicion of being a traitor to his country. Alex Villaplane led France out against Mexico in the opening match to the inaugural 1930 World Cup and, after helping France to a 4–1 victory, proclaimed it to be the proudest day of his life. Fifteen years later, Villaplane was shot by the French Resistance for allegedly collaborating with the Nazis during the Second World War.

QUIET NIGHT

When England entertained Malta in 1971, the Maltese failed to force even a goal-kick or a corner during the 90 minutes and Gordon Banks in the England goal didn't have a single shot to save. The four occasions on which he touched the ball were all from back-passes. England won 5–0. Chris Woods enjoyed a similar experience when England defeated San Marino 6–0 in a World Cup qualifier at Wembley on 17 February 1993. Like Banks before him, Woods didn't have a shot to save. He touched the ball just six times in the entire match.

EFFENBERG OFF

Aptly named German midfielder Stefan Effenberg was sent home from the 1994 World Cup finals in the United States after showing his middle finger to German fans during his country's unconvincing 3–2 victory over South Korea.

BRAZIL NUTS

The final of the 1950 World Cup in Brazil was watched by a record crowd of 199,850. They saw Uruguay defeat Brazil 2–1.

LOST IN THE TRANSLATION

The Albanian national team were sent packing from England in 1990 after going on an illegal shopping spree at Heathrow. The problems arose when the 37-strong squad, who were on their way to Reykjavik for a European Chamionships qualifier with Iceland, misinterpreted "Duty Free" as meaning "Help Yourself". Laden with watches, the Albanians were apprehended by police before they could board their plane. The stolen property was recovered and no charges were pressed on condition that the players left Britain on the next available flight.

TWO GARY STEVENS . . .

At the 1986 World Cup finals, England fielded two defenders by the name of Gary Stevens – one who played for Spurs, the other for Everton. This led to the England fans' chant: "Two Gary Stevens . . . There's only two Gary Stevens."

BY ROYAL APPOINTMENT

The Romanian team for the 1930 World Cup was

selected personally by King Carol II. At first the Romanian Football Association had declined an invitation to take part in the tournament but the football-mad king intervened and arranged for the players to have up to three months off work with full pay. Romania were eliminated after just two matches.

THE GAME NO ONE WANTED TO WIN

The 1998 Tiger Cup – a bi-annual tournament for Asian countries – descended into farce as opponents Indonesia and Thailand both desperately tried to lose the same game. By the time the two nations met in their final Group A fixture, both had already qualified for the semi-finals, but the winners would have to meet hosts Vietnam in the intimidating setting of Hanoi. Neither Indonesia nor Thailand wanted to face Vietnam so both set out to lose. The two teams failed to mount a serious attack in the first half but, following an interval warning from the match commissioner, things perked up in the second period. Indonesia led twice but Thailand equalised in the 89th minute. Then with the seconds ticking away, the Indonesia defenders played keep-ball on the edge of their penalty area until Mursyid Effendi suddenly strode up and hammered the ball into his own net which had deliberately been left unguarded by the keeper. To the despair of the Thai players, there was no time left for them to give away an equaliser. As 3–2 winners, they had to go to Hanoi. Their fears about the trip were not unfounded, Vietnam running out the 3–0 winners. But Indonesia didn't profit from their chicanery either. In their semi-final they lost 2–1 to Singapore. Indonesia and Thailand were each fined £25,000 by the Asian Confederation.

FIRST BLANK

England's 0–0 draw with Scotland in 1970 was the first goalless game between the two sides since their very first meeting back in 1872.

SHORTEST MATCH

When Estonia failed to turn up for their World Cup qualifying tie with Scotland in Tallinn in 1996, the resultant match was just about the shortest on record. Scotland lined up, kicked off and the referee blew the final whistle after just three seconds of "play". The fixture was subsequently replayed.

SWITCHED SIDES

England forward Stan Mortensen actually made his international debut against England! He was one of the England reserves on duty for the 1943 wartime international against Wales at Wembley and when the Welsh lost wing-half Ivor Powell through injury, England generously agreed to let Mortensen take his place.

GOULD GETS SHIRTY

Leicester City midfielder Robbie Savage was dropped from the Welsh squad by manager Bobby Gould in 1998 as punishment for disrespectfully throwing away Paolo Maldini's Italy shirt during a TV interview in the build-up to the game between the two countries. Savage was later reinstated to the squad as a substitute. Wales lost the European Championship qualifier 2–0 and Savage ended up apologising to Maldini.

TOOK MATTERS INTO HIS OWN HANDS

Following a 2–1 win in Haiti in the first leg of a 1970 World Cup qualifying tie, El Salvador were supremely confident of making it to the finals in Mexico. But for the second leg, Haiti's entourage included a witch doctor who sprinkled some powder on the pitch, chanted a spell and saw Haiti move into a three-goal lead by half-time. So it went to a play-off in Kingston, Jamaica. There El Salvador's Argentinian coach Gregorio Bundio literally took matters into his own hands by punching the witch doctor and putting an end to his spells. El Salvador won 1–0.

GREEK TRAGEDY

Only 651 spectators bothered to turn up to watch Greece's European Championship qualifier with Hungary on 3 December 1983.

ENGLAND SPECTACLE

James Frederick Mitchell of Manchester City is the only goalkeeper to have played for England wearing glasses. He won his solitary cap against Northern Ireland in 1925. The game ended in a goalless draw.

HALCYON DAYS

In a seven-month spell between October 1960 and May 1961, England, managed by Walter Winterbottom, won six internationals on the trot, scoring 40 goals in the process. The sequence started on 8 October with a 5–2 win over Northern Ireland in Belfast and was followed 11 days later by a 9–0 victory in Luxembourg in a World Cup qualifier. A week on, and Spain were beaten 4–2 at Wembley. On 23 November Wales were despatched 5–1 at Wembley which, on 15 April, then became the setting for Scotland's greatest humiliation at the hands of the "Auld Enemy" – the famous 9–3 defeat. Finally on 10 May, England put eight past Mexico at Wembley without reply.

FIRST HOME DEFEATS

Although in 1953 Hungary were the first non-British team to beat England at Wembley, they were not the first to taste victory on English soil. Four years previously the Republic of Ireland had defeated England 2–0 at Goodison Park.

ALWAYS THERE

Brazil are the only country to have played in the final stages of every World Cup.

NOT SO FRIENDLY

A so-called "friendly" between Scotland and Austria at Hampden Park on 8 May 1963 was abandoned by referee Jim Finney after 79 minutes to prevent further injury. By that time, two Austrians had been sent off and one carried off. Scotland were leading 4–1.

TURNED THE OTHER CHEEK

As he slotted home the penalty against Brazil that secured Italy a place in the 1938 World Cup Final, Peppino Meazza noticed that his shorts, which had been torn earlier in the game, had slipped down to his ankles. His celebrating team-mates crowded round him to spare his blushes until a fresh pair were brought on.

GREAVSIE AND GROMIT

A dog ran on to the pitch and urinated over Jimmy Greaves during England's game with Brazil in the 1962 World Cup finals in Chile.

SPARED JAIL

By holding Gambia to a goalless draw in 1980, Liberia players escaped imprisonment. The Liberian Head of State, Master Sergeant Samuel Doe, had threatened to jail them if they lost.

ONE-CLUB TEAM

Anderlecht supplied all 11 players for Belgium's international with Holland on 30 September 1964.

FIRST, SECOND AND THIRD

West Germany's Wolfgang Overath finished first, second and third in the World Cup . . . but not in that order. He was a member of the German team beaten by England in the 1966 final and in 1970 he scored the only goal of the third place play-off against Uruguay. Then in 1974 came his moment of glory when he starred in the 2–1 victory over Holland.

THE NAKED TRUTH

When a woman named Rosemary Mello threw a flare on to the pitch during a 1990 World Cup qualifier between Chile and Brazil, it had unexpected repercussions. Chile were banned from the next World Cup; their goalkeeper, Rojas, feigned injury to such an extent that he was banned for life; and Ms Mello went on to appear nude in *Playboy* magazine.

A CHANGE OF HEART

Frustrated at being overlooked in favour of Ray Clemence, Peter Shilton pulled out of the England squad in 1976 and asked not to be considered for future selection. At the time Shilton had won 21 caps. Three months later he changed his mind and went on to win 125 caps.

CUP FOUND BY DOG

A week after the World Cup had been stolen from Central Hall, Westminster, where it was on display prior to the 1966 competition, it was found wrapped in brown paper in a clump of bushes in a Norwood garden. The discovery was made by a dog named Pickles who relished becoming an overnight celebrity. While his owner, David Corbett, got the £6000 reward, Pickles received the ultimate accolade of being invited to the celebration banquet following England's win in the final.

UNORTHODOX APPROACH

Iran players prepared for a 1998 World Cup tie versus Yugoslavia with a three-hour session of mourning in memory of a seventh-century Shiite Moslem saint. The players beat their chests and wept till midnight while a teacher recounted the saint's death. The unusual preparations failed to have the desired effect, however, since Iran lost 1–0 the next day.

ALPINE HEAT

After going down 7–5 to Austria in a quarter-final

match in the 1954 World Cup, hosts Switzerland blamed their defeat on the hot weather. It emerged that their normally reliable goalkeeper Eugene Parlier had been suffering from sunstroke.

GARY'S GAFFE

Needing just one goal to equal Bobby Charlton's England total of 49 goals, Gary Lineker was presented with a golden opportunity when England were awarded a penalty against Brazil on 17 May 1992. He tried to chip the ball cheekily over the keeper but instead sent it gently into his arms. England drew the game 1–1 and Lineker, who won only four more caps, was left marooned on 48 goals.

FIRST FOOTER

When Charlton Athletic's John Hewie made his international debut for the Scots against England at Hampden Park in 1956, it was the first time that the South African-born forward had actually set foot in Scotland.

HUNGARY FOR SUCCESS

Hungary remained unbeaten at home in senior internationals for 17 years. On 8 June 1939 they lost 3–1 to Italy but did not taste defeat again on Hungarian soil until 20 May 1956 when Czechoslovakia stunned them 4–2.

SEVEN GUNNERS

Arsenal supplied seven of the England team which faced Italy at Highbury in 1935 – Frank Moss, George Male, Eddie Hapgood, Wilf Copping, Ray Bowden, Ted Drake and Cliff Bastin. In 1977, six of the England team which took the field against Switzerland at Wembley played for Liverpool.

OVERPOWERED BY FANS

After Brazil had lifted the 1970 World Cup, one of their heroes, Rivelino, was mobbed by fans. He collapsed under the weight of their congratulations and had to be stretchered off to the dressing-room.

THEY CALLED HIM ERNIE . . .

In the 1978 World Cup semi-final with Italy, Holland's Ernie Brandts succeeded in scoring an own goal, accidentally knocking out his own goalkeeper and scoring his side's equaliser in their 2–1 win.

THE TEAM THAT JACK BUILT

Under Jack Charlton, the Republic of Ireland played

England four times and didn't lose once. They won one game and drew the other three.

ONE-ARMED GERMAN

Stuttgart centre-half and captain Robert Schlienz won three caps for West Germany in the 1950s despite the handicap of having only one arm.

SCORING SEQUENCES

Tinsley Lindley of Cambridge University scored in nine consecutive internationals for England between 1886 and 1888. In more recent times, Ipswich's Paul Mariner scored in six consecutive England internationals between November 1981 and June 1982.

CHANGED NATIONALITIES

Luis Monti appeared in two consecutive World Cup Finals . . . but for two different countries. In 1930 he played for the Argentine team which lost out to Uruguay, but he enjoyed better fortune four years later when he was a member of the Italian side which lifted the trophy at the expense of Czechoslovakia.

FLYING DUTCHMEN

West Germany went a goal down to Holland in the

1974 World Cup Final before they had even touched the ball. Straight from the kick-off the Dutch strung together a move of 15 passes which culminated in Johan Cruyff being brought down in the box by Uli Hoeness. British referee Jack Taylor pointed to the spot and Johan Neeskens converted the kick with barely a minute gone. But the Germans fought back to win 2–1.

ALL WHITE

Romania's players all bleached their hair at the end of the first round matches in the 1998 World Cup finals to celebrate reaching the second stage. The only one who didn't was their goalkeeper who was completely bald.

SWAP STOPPED

The Albanian FA refused to allow Albania's players to swap shirts with opponents Spain at the end of a 1993 international because it couldn't afford to buy replacements.

WHY IRISH EYES ARE SMILING

Strange as it may seem, but Northern Ireland are the holders of the Home International Championship. Although England won the championship a record 34 times in its 100-year existence and shared it on a further 20 occasions, the last tournament in 1984 was won by the Irish with Wales in second place.

BETTER LATE THAN NEVER

Until 1994 the fastest goal in the World Cup finals was credited to Bryan Robson who scored in 27 seconds against France in Spain in 1982. Then, acting on a tip-off from a TV researcher, FIFA awarded the accolade to Vaclav Masek who scored in 15 seconds for Czechoslovakia against Mexico in Chile in 1962. So Masek entered the record books 32 years after the event.

RAVELLI'S RECORD

Sweden goalkeeper Thomas Ravelli holds the record for the greatest number of international caps. He played for his country 143 times between 1981 and 1997. The record holders for England, Wales and Northern Ireland are goalkeepers too – Peter Shilton (125 caps), Neville Southall (92) and Pat Jennings (119) respectively. The only one of the home countries whose most-capped man is an outfield player is Scotland where Kenny Dalglish leads the way with 102 appearances.

OPTED OUT

After winning the inaugural World Cup in Argentina in 1930, Uruguay didn't bother travelling to Italy to defend it four years later.

DEFECTED

Three members of the Afghanistan national team defected to India in 1984.

FIRST FOR FAEROES

In September 1990 the tiny Faeroe Islands gained a famous victory in their first-ever competitive international by beating Austria 1–0 in a European Championship qualifier. Although it was a home game for the islanders, it had to be played in Sweden since there were only artificial pitches on the Faeroes. The result was such a blow to Austrian pride that manager Josef Hickersberger promptly resigned.

UNBEATEN FOR OVER TWO YEARS

Brazil hold the record for the longest unbeaten run in international football. From December 1993, they went 37 matches without defeat until losing 2–0 to Mexico in the CONCACAF Gold Cup Final on 21 January 1996.

EIGHT-MINUTE CAREER

After just eight minutes of his England debut against Northern Ireland on 19 October 1929, West Ham's

Jimmy Barrett was carried off injured. He was never picked for his country again.

NAME CHANGE

Before becoming a full international with Wales, in 1989 Ryan Giggs played for England Under-18s as Ryan Wilson, the surname being that of his father, a former Welsh Rugby League player.

ALL FOUR QUALIFIED

The only time all four home international countries have qualified for the final stages of the World Cup was in 1958. Wales and Northern Ireland went the furthest, both reaching the quarter-finals.

IRAQI HORROR

Nine Iraqi fans were killed and 120 wounded by jubilant supporters after their country's World Cup victory over China in 1993.

TRAGIC KILLING

On returning home to Colombia following his side's shock exit from the 1994 World Cup finals, national captain Andres Escobar was shot dead. His crime had been to score an own goal in his country's defeat to the

United States – a result which effectively put the
Colombians out of the competition.

FIRST AND LAST

Stanley Matthews scored his first goal for England,
against Wales on 29 September 1934 and his last against
Northern Ireland on 6 October 1956. The 22-year gap is
the longest between a British international's first and
last goals for his country.

DOCTOR'S ORDERS

Dr Bob Mills-Roberts insisted on keeping goal for Wales
against England in 1897 even though movement was
virtually impossible because his arms were in splints up
to the elbows. In the circumstances, he did well to keep
the final score down to 4–0.

FIVE IN A ROW

Goalkeeper Antonio Carbajal of Mexico appeared in the
final stages of five successive World Cups between 1950
and 1966, a record that has since been equalled by
Germany's midfielder Lothar Matthäus.

PERUVIAN RIOT

Over 300 people were killed in rioting in the Peruvian

capital Lima after Peru had seen a goal disallowed against Argentina in May 1964.

SENT HOME

Controversial Scottish winger Willie Johnston was sent home in disgrace from South America after testing positive for drugs at the 1978 World Cup finals. Johnston tested positive for Fencamfamine, contained in a flu remedy he had taken to help him sleep better.

PELE SHOWS THE WAY

The longest unbeaten run in World Cup finals is 13 games by Brazil. After winning the tournament in 1958 and 1962, they were finally kicked off the park by Hungary in 1966. Brazil also hold the claim to being the only country ever to win the World Cup outside their continent. They won in Sweden in 1958. And Brazilian star Pele is the only player to have been a member of three World Cup winning sides – in 1958, 1962 and 1970.

PLAYED FOR THREE COUNTRIES

Ladislav Kubala is the only player to have played for three different countries at international level. He represented Hungary three times, Czechoslovakia 11 times, and Spain 19 times.

MISSED HIS TRAIN

Selected to play for England against Scotland in 1875, Bill Carr missed his train and arrived late for the kick-off. He took the field for the last 75 minutes but was never picked for his country again.

ALL-ROUNDER

Andy Goram represented Scotland at football and cricket. In addition to keeping goal for his country, he won the first of his three cricketing caps in 1989 against the touring Australians.

JUST BEATEN

Just Fontaine of France holds the record for the most number of goals in a single World Cup tournament. He scored 13 in six matches in the 1958 tournament. But the highest goalscorer in the history of World Cup finals is West Germany's Gerd Muller. He scored a total of 14 goals – 10 in 1970 and another four in 1974.

THE WRIGHT STUFF

Wolves and England centre-half Billy Wright played in

70 consecutive internationals between October 1951 and May 1959. He won a total of 105 caps in all.

COINING IT

Spain won two international championships on the toss of a coin. They were awarded the International Youth Championships in 1952 and 1954 by calling correctly after the final had ended in a draw.

MULLER MAGIC

Gerd Möller, West Germany's ace marksman of the 1970s, scored an amazing 68 goals in 62 appearances for his country.

BOBBY DAZZLER

Robert Prosinecki became the first player to score for two different countries in the World Cup when he netted for Croatia against Jamaica in the 1998 finals. Eight years earlier, he had scored for Yugoslavia.

OLE OLEG

Oleg Salenko of Russia is the only player to score five goals in a match in the World Cup finals. His contribution helped Russia thrash Cameroon 6–1 in 1994.

PASTA MASTERS

England's proud 48-year-old record of never having lost a World Cup qualifying match at home came to an end in 1997 when Italy won 1–0 at Wembley.

SAMBA TIME

The only player to score in every match of the World Cup finals was Jairzinho of Brazil who scored seven goals in six games in 1970.

CZECHS CASHED IN

When Scotland lost 2–1 to the Czech Republic in a European Championship qualifier at Celtic Park on 31 March 1999, it was their first home defeat in a competitive international for 12 years.

PEARCE'S CLANGER

The fastest international goal on record is one Stuart Pearce would rather forget. For it was his under-hit back-pass which allowed Davide Gualtieri to score for San Marino after just 8.3 seconds of the World Cup qualifier in Bologna on 17 November 1993.

HIGH SCORERS

The highest score in a World Cup match is the 17 which Iran put past The Maldives in a qualifying tie in May 1997. The highest score in the finals is the ten which Hungary netted against El Salvador in 1982.

HOSTS WITH THE LEAST

In the 16 World Cups to date, only six host nations have failed to reached the semi-finals – France (1938), Switzerland (1954), Mexico (1970), Spain (1982), Mexico (1986) and USA (1994).

CON ARTIST

Chilean captain and goalkeeper Roberto Rojas was banned for life by FIFA after faking injury during a 1989 World Cup qualifier against Brazil. With Chile losing 1–0, Rojas went down claiming he had been hit by a flare. The Chile players fled from the pitch and the match was abandoned but when the duplicity was uncovered, Brazil were awarded the game and Chile were banned from taking part in the 1994 World Cup.

GREAT DANES

Denmark won the 1992 European Championship . . . despite not qualifying. After Yugoslavia withdrew at

the 11th hour following the outbreak of civil war,
Denmark were invited to take their place. And the
unfancied Danes went all the way, defeating Germany in the final.

THE MIGHTY MAGYARS

Between 1950 and 1956, Hungary lost only once in 48
internationals – and that was against West Germany in
the 1954 World Cup Final. Ironically, Hungary had
earlier hammered the Germans 8–3 in a group match.

COLE'S QUARTET

Andy Cole won his first four England caps under four
different managers – Terry Venables, Glenn Hoddle,
Howard Wilkinson and Kevin Keegan.

STAYED AT HOME

Although they qualified for the final stages of the 1950
World Cup, Scotland declined the invitation to go to
Brazil. India also withdrew from the 1950 finals because
FIFA refused to allow them to play barefoot!

BULGARIAN BLITZ

After appearing in five World Cup finals (1962, 1966,
1970, 1974 and 1986) without winning a single match,

Bulgaria suddenly struck gold in the 1994 tournament. They got off the mark with a 4–0 victory over Greece and eventually reached the semi-finals, their most celebrated scalp being that of the Germans at the quarter-final stage.

SUPER MARIO

Two people have won the World Cup both as player and manager. Mario Zagalo was a member of the victorious Brazilian teams of 1958 and 1962 and he managed the side which won in 1970. Franz Beckenbauer was captain of the West German team which won in 1974 and was the German manager when they won again in 1990.

A DIFFERENT BALL GAME

In the 1930 World Cup Final, Argentina and Uruguay could not reach an agreement on which ball to use. So they played the first half with Argentina's ball and the second half with Uruguay's. The switch was decisive. For, after trailing at half-time, Uruguay warmed to their own ball and ran out 4–2 winners.

ROOKIE NEVILLE

Gary Neville had played only 19 first-team games for Manchester United when he was selected to play for England against Japan in 1995.

COME ON, EILEEN!

In April 1998 unofficial England team faith-healer Eileen Drewery revealed that she stopped Ian Wright scoring in the World Cup qualifier in Italy the previous October (he had hit the post in the last minute) for fear that the goal would have incited crowd trouble.

STATESIDE STUNNER

When England lost 1–0 to the United States in the 1950 World Cup, the result came as such a shock that back home the English press thought it was a misprint for 1–10.

SORRY SCOTS

Scotland have qualified for the final stages of the World Cup on eight occasions but have yet to get past the first round. Alex Ferguson acted as caretaker-manager for Scotland in the 1986 tournament in Mexico following the sudden death of Jock Stein during Scotland's last qualifying match against Wales.

FLUSHED OUT

In August 1998, a judge in Rio de Janeiro, ruling on an action brought by Mario Zagallo, ordered Brazilian star Romario to remove a huge caricature of the former national coach from the toilet door of a bar he owned.

HURST STRIKES AGAIN

When England's 1966 World Cup team beat their West German counterparts 6–4 in 1985 in a match in aid of the victims of the Bradford City fire, 46-year-old Geoff Hurst repeated his hat-trick of 19 years earlier.

19

HOME AND AWAY

THANKSGIVING TREK

At the end of the 1968–9 season, the entire Sampdoria team plus 200 fans walked 20 miles to a mountain sanctuary near Genoa to thank the Madonna for saving them from relegation. A 1–1 draw with Juventus in the final match enabled them to keep their place in the top division.

BIG BREAK

The half-time interval at the Perugia–Juventus match on 14 May 2000 lasted an incredible 82 minutes while the referee waited for water to clear off the pitch following a sudden deluge. When the game eventually restarted, Perugia went on to snatch a shock victory – a result which cost Juventus the Serie "A" title.

WIVES ON THE WARPATH

In an attempt to keep the team fresh before a big Cup Final in 1964, the Apia club of Sydney tried to isolate the players at a secret retreat for three days in the build-up to the game. However, the players' wives objected and refused to let them go. In the end the club backed down for the sake of domestic harmony.

THE SOUND OF SILENCE

Following an outbreak of hooliganism among both players and supporters on the run-in to the 1964 Algerian League Championship, the country banned spectators from all matches for the rest of the season.

MP TORE STRIP OFF GAZZA

During his stint with Lazio in 1993, Gazza incurred the wrath of an Italian MP for belching into a microphone.

THE PLOT SICKENS

A French team from Sully-sur-Loire near Orleans tried to stave off relegation by lacing the visiting side's lemonade with knock-out drops. With players collapsing all around, it didn't take the referee long to spot that something was amiss. The offending club were duly reported to the authorities. Their punishment? Relegation.

BIG FIX

No fewer than 185 Hungarian players were suspended in a purge in the early 1980s following accusations of fixing matches on pools coupons.

DEMON DAMIAN

Damian Mori scored for Adelaide City after just four seconds of an Australian National League game with Sydney United on 6 December 1995.

LOW SCORERS

AIK Stockholm captured the Swedish League title in 1999 despite scoring just 25 goals in 26 matches.

A DANGEROUS PRECEDENT?

The German FA ordered a 1994 Bundesliga match

between Bayern Munich and Nuremberg to be replayed after TV evidence showed that the referee had awarded Bayern a goal even though the ball had clearly not crossed the line. How long before the Germans insist on replaying the 1966 World Cup Final?

MONEY-BACK GUARANTEE

Having seen his side go eight matches without a win in 1998 and gates fall alarmingly, Kleber Leite, president of Brazilian giants Flamengo, guaranteed that all supporters who attended the home game with Portuguesa would get their money back if Flamengo lost again. A crowd of 52,340 took up the offer (compared to the previous home gate of 791) but it proved a costly exercise as Flamengo lost 3–2 after twice being ahead.

MOTTY BEWARE!

After a match in Lima, a TV interviewer asked strapping Peruvian striker Corina why he had missed three simple headed chances and how he thought that area of his game could be improved. Corina deliberated for a moment and then announced "like this", whereupon he head-butted his inquisitor in the face. Corina was arrested by police following a scuffle.

THE DIVINE PONYTAIL

Nicknamed "Il Codino Divino" (The Divine Ponytail), Roberto Baggio was so popular with Fiorentina fans that when he was transferred to Juventus in 1990, irate supporters of the Florence club rioted for three days. Playing against Fiorentina the following year, Baggio was substituted for refusing to take a penalty against his old club.

BAR TO SUCCESS

Spanish Third Division club Castellon couldn't understand why they found it easier to score away from home in 1995–6 . . . until they measured their goals and found that their crossbars were eight inches too low.

KIDNAPPED

Zimbabwe striker Elisha Banda, who played for air force team Cone Textiles, was kidnapped, drugged and tortured for eight days in 1986 by air force colleagues. He was eventually found bound and gagged on scrubland near Harare. His team-mates had been angry that their star player had signed for a civilian team.

FAMILY MAN

Following a series of offensive undershirt revelations, Italian authorities feared the worst when Parma's Argentinian striker Hernando Crespo lifted his shirt after scoring in 1999. Instead all he revealed were photos of his niece and nephew.

PRESIDENTIAL PLEA

Croatian goalkeeper Drazen Ladic came out of retirement from international football in 1998 in response to a personal plea from State President Franjo Tudjman.

LEAVING IT LATE

Barcelona certainly believed in taking things to the wire in the early 1990s. When they won the Spanish League in 1994, it was the third year in succession that they had clinched the title in the closing minutes of the last day of the season.

NET RESULT

In 1971, Borussia Moenchengladbach were entertaining Werder Bremen in the West German Bundesliga. With two minutes to go and the score at 1–1, one of the goals collapsed. The match was abandoned and Borussia were made to forfeit the game as they were deemed responsible for not having replacement goal apparatus. Since they were leading the League at the time, the decision could have had serious repercussions, but they managed to hold on to claim the title anyway.

SELF-SERVICE

Seven players from Mozambique's Costa do Sol club were banned for life in 1998 after being caught shoplifting during a trip to Portugal for an African Cup Winners' Cup tie in Casablanca.

TWO LITTLE PIGS

After pulling off a shock 3–2 victory over Croatia Zagreb in the Croatian National Cup in 1998, little Fourth Division club Dugo Selo couldn't afford to pay their players the promised win bonus of £38 each until the directors had sold a pair of pigs.

DINO SORE

Goalkeeper Dino Zoff went on to play 112 times for Italy and captained his country to victory in the 1982 World Cup. Yet on his League debut for Udinese back in 1961, he let in five goals.

NIGHT IN JAIL

In 1973 an entire team of Galilee players spent the night in an Israeli jail for kicking their opponents in a 3–1 defeat.

BLOWING THEIR OWN TRUMPET

FC Nürnberg filed an official protest with the German FA in 1999 after losing 3–0 at Dortmund because, they claimed, the crowd were too noisy. Nürnberg maintained that their players "had been unable to concentrate on the game". The problem had been caused by a sponsor distributing 40,000 toy trumpets to the Dortmund supporters which they squeaked whenever Nürnberg attacked.

CANTONA AXED

Eric Cantona was banned from international football for a year in 1990 for insulting the French national team manager Henri Michel.

DOWNHILL ALL THE WAY

Bayern Munich star Lothar Matthäus had trouble on three fronts in the autumn of 1998. First he tore a thigh muscle in the 2–2 draw with Borussia Dortmund and then he was tackled by the Swiss authorities who threatened to seize his alpine chalet unless he paid £600 due in back taxes. Finally he was fined by Bayern for going skiing while he was supposed to be resting his injury!

ALBANIAN BOYCOTT

In the wake of a brawl between players and fans and an

attack on the referee, Skenderbeu decided to boycott the Albanian League. The incidents occurred during Skenderbeu's 3–2 victory over leaders Vllaznia in 1998 and led to Albania's Soccer Federation overturning the result and awarding the game to Vllaznia. The loss of the three points dropped Skenderbeu from ninth place to bottom of the table and when an appeal failed, they refused to show up for the next game.

NOT THE FOGGIEST

For their tour to London in 1945–6, Moscow Dynamo laid down strict conditions. They insisted on eating all meals at the Soviet Embassy and demanded that they be allowed to provide their own referee for at least one of the games. The Russian referee duly took charge of the friendly with Arsenal, played at White Hart Lane because Highbury was being rebuilt after the war. But the fog was so thick that the referee patrolled one touchline with his two English linesmen on the other touchline. And none of the crowd had the foggiest idea what the score was.

LOSING STREAK

Paulo Mata, coach with Itaperuna of Brazil, was so angry at a referee for allowing a late goal against his team in 1997 then sending off three of his players, that he rushed on to the pitch towards the official. On the way, Mata pulled off his shirt before being stopped in his tracks by three policemen. Prevented from reaching the referee, Mata contented himself with dropping his trousers and mooning at the TV cameras.

NEVER CAN SAY GOODBYE

Palermo player Graziano Landoni was fined £670 in 1971 for refusing to say goodbye to the club's trainer.

QUICK-FIRE COLOMBIANS

Three goals were scored in just 75 seconds in a Colombian League match in 1998. Visitors Bucaramanga took the lead, only for opponents Cortulua to equalise 30 seconds later and then take a sensational lead within another 45 seconds. Both goals came from Jairo Hurtado. But Bucaramanga had the last word and snatched a 2–2 draw.

OVER-EXPOSED

Weather conditions were so appalling during an Irish Cup tie between Ards and Coleraine in February 1967 that a number of players collapsed from exposure to the bitter cold and driving rain.

THREE-DAY RELEASE

Alfredo di Stefano was kidnapped while on a tour of

Venezuela with Real Madrid in 1963 but was released unharmed three days later.

SELF-INFLICTED WOUND

African police were overcome by their own tear gas as they tried to break up a fight at the end of Gor Mahia's 1–0 victory over AFC Leopards in 1987. As a result, they were unable to arrest anyone.

REFEREES IN BRAWL

A game between two teams of referees in Spain should have been just about the best-behaved fixture on the calendar. But it ended in uproar after the match official sent one off and was promptly felled by a blow from the disgraced player's father, also a referee.

HINT OF CORRUPTION

In 1979, Yugoslav team Illinden FC needed a big victory from their final match to boost their goal difference sufficiently to win promotion. Somehow they managed to persuade their opponents, Mladost, and the referee to help them out, with the result that Illinden finished up winning 134–1. Presumably the goal against was to make it look genuine. They might have got away with it too had their promotion rivals not practised similar skulduggery, arranging their match to finish 88–0.

BORROWED CUP

A group of Lorraine steelworkers "borrowed" the Coupe de France (the French equivalent of the FA Cup) from Nantes FC in 1979 as part of a campaign to save the steel mills. The Cup was returned to Nantes four days later.

20

THE MANAGEMENT

MASTER OF DISGUISE

Under threat from Burnley fans who still had bitter memories of his time in charge at Turf Moor, Shrewsbury manager John Bond disguised himself in a steward's uniform to watch the December 1992 meeting between the two clubs from the back of the stand. It was not a happy return for Bond who saw Shrewsbury lose 2–1 to two goals in the last four minutes.

SCALING THE HEIGHTS

In the build-up to Colchester United's epic FA Cup tie with mighty Leeds in 1971, the Fourth Division club's manager Dick Graham promised to scale the walls of Colchester Castle if his team pulled off the biggest Cup upset in years. And after Leeds had been humbled 3–2, Graham kept his word and climbed the castle walls on the Thursday after the match.

HAT TRICK

Lincoln City manager/chairman John Reames was so delighted at his side's victory over Northampton Town in January 1999 that he threw his hat into the air in celebration. But when he went to retrieve it, the hat had vanished. Two days later he received a ransom note which read: "Put £100 into the players' pool or you'll never see your hat again!"

MANAGER OF THE WEEK

Bill Lambton was manager of Scunthorpe United for only three days in April 1958. He saw his team play just once, losing 3–0 to Liverpool at Anfield. But even that was more than Steve Murray achieved at Forfar Athletic in 1980. He stayed as manager for just five days before resigning without even seeing the side play. Swansea City manager Kevin Cullis resigned in February 1996 after just seven days in charge. Cullis – a surprise choice having previously been manager of Cradley Town – called the Swansea club "a shambles". The players responded by complaining that they had been given "a pub team manager". The following year, Swansea had another short-term manager when Micky Adams stayed just 13 days at the Vetch Field.

A CUTTING REMARK

When Daniel Passarella became coach of the Argentine national team following the 1994 World Cup, he immediately announced that he would not select any players with long hair.

SACKED EIGHT TIMES

During the troubled reign of chairman Stan Flashman in the early 1990s, Barnet manager Barry Fry was officially sacked on no fewer than eight occasions. But each time he was reinstated shortly afterwards. The colourful Fry was at it again in May 2000, claiming that he had been sacked by Peterborough United just four days after leading them to promotion from Division Three. The following day Fry returned to the club, saying it had all been a misunderstanding.

NO FUTCHER

When Paul Futcher took over as manager of Darlington in 1995, he had to wait eight games before seeing his team score. Even then Paul Olsen's header was merely a prelude to a 2–1 defeat at Scunthorpe. Two games later, and still looking for his first win, Futcher stepped down.

THE FAMOUS FOUR

Only four managers have won the League Championship with different clubs – Tom Watson (with Sunderland and Liverpool), Herbert Chapman (with Huddersfield Town and Arsenal), Brian Clough (with Derby County and Nottingham Forest) and Kenny Dalglish (with Liverpool and Blackburn Rovers). Dalglish also became the first person to win the League and Cup "double" as a player-manager when he led Liverpool in 1985–6.

MOB RULE

Jimmy Mullen quit as boss of Burnley in 1996 after thugs set fire to his wife's dress in a Chinese takeaway.

FOWL PLAY

Fred Westgarth, who managed Hartlepool United from 1943 to 1957, used to keep his chickens in the rafters of the main stand of the Victoria Ground. He would take them home on the eve of a match and bring them back to the ground on Monday mornings.

SUPER DARIO

Of current Football League managers, Dario Gradi of Crewe Alexandra has been longest with the same club. He has been in charge at Gresty Road since June 1983. In second place (and the longest-serving Premiership manager) is Sir Alex Ferguson who has been at Old Trafford since November 1986. Third is Wrexham's Brian Flynn, appointed in November 1989.

ALL WHITE

On taking over as Leeds United manager in 1962, Don Revie changed the club strip to all white in the hope that they could be as successful as Real Madrid. Then in

1967, Millwall manager Benny Fenton switched the Lions' strip to all white in the hope that a bit of the Real and Leeds magic would rub off on South London.

FAMILY FEUD

Roy McDonough was sacked as manager of Colchester United in 1994 by club chairman Gordon Parker . . . who also happened to be his father-in-law.

BOB'S BEST

With 20 trophies for Liverpool between 1974 and 1983, Bob Paisley remains the most successful English-club manager of all time. In that period, he won six League Championships, three European Champions' Cups, three Football League Cups, one UEFA Cup, one European Super Cup and six Charity Shields (one shared). The only prize that eluded him, as it did Brian Clough, was the FA Cup. Paisley was associated with Liverpool for 57 years in all. He joined the club from Bishop Auckland in 1939 and, until his death in 1996, served them as player, trainer, coach, assistant manager, manager, director and vice-president.

TOP DOG

Sir Alex Ferguson is the most successful manager with Scottish and English clubs combined. During his eight-year reign at Aberdeen from 1978 to 1986, he picked up ten major prizes – three Scottish Championships, four

Scottish FA Cups, one Scottish League Cup, one European Cup Winners' Cup and one European Super Cup. In the past 11 seasons with Manchester United, he has captured 13 major trophies – six League Championships, four FA Cups, one League Cup, one UEFA Champions' League and one European Cup Winners' Cup.

SEVILLE WAR

Spanish club Betis Sevilla had three different managers before a ball had been kicked at the start of the 1998–9 season. Luis Aragones walked out in July and was replaced by Antonio Oliveira from FC Porto of Portugal. But Oliveira too resigned 22 days later and so, just three days before kick-off, Betis had their third manager in quick succession – Argentinian-born Vicente Cantatore. Even then the omens weren't good – the previous season Cantatore had walked out on Sporting Lisbon after only one game in charge.

RUFFLED BIRD'S FEATHERS

York City manager John Bird and his Scarborough counterpart Ray McHale were sent off following a touchline fracas in 1989. Tempers became heated in the wake of a foul on Scarborough midfielder Paul Dobson and the two managers squared up to each other before trying to trade punches. Both were subsequently banned from the touchline for three months. York won the match 3–1.

NO ROOM FOR SENTIMENT

Sheffield Wednesday goalscoring legend Derek Dooley had to have a leg amputated following an injury sustained during a match. He later became the club's manager but was sacked on Christmas Eve 1973.

LAST-MINUTE REPLACEMENT

When a trialist cried off at the last minute, Preston manager Gary Peters turned out for the club's reserves against Mansfield Town Reserves in 1995. Forty-year-old Peters played at centre-half and steered Preston to a 6–0 victory.

CHURCH BELL

Former Leeds United full-back Willie Bell resigned from his job as Lincoln City boss in October 1978 to join a religious sect in America.

BOOTED OUT

Ilie Balaci, coach with Romanian club Universitatea Craiova, was banned for a year after striking the referee with a boot following a 1–0 home defeat by Otelul Galati on 30 August 1998.

NO EXPERIENCE NECESSARY

Neither Crewe Alexandra boss Dario Gradi nor Luton Town manager Lennie Lawrence ever played League football. Barnsley's Dave Bassett played only 35 games for Wimbledon (having previously been rejected by both Watford and Chelsea) while Lawrie McMenemy had but a short playing career with Gateshead.

ARSENAL ODDITY

George Allison, the ex-journalist who steered Arsenal to League Championships in 1935 and 1938 and FA Cup success in 1936, never played League football. And Bertie Mee, the manager who led Arsenal to the double in 1971, only had a very brief playing career as a winger with Mansfield Town before being forced to retire at the age of 27 through injury.

DAPPER DAVE

Chelsea manager Dave Sexton insisted on wearing the same overcoat on match days throughout his team's 1970 FA Cup run, regardless of the weather. He also wore a blazer with a button missing and refused to let his wife sew one on until Chelsea were knocked out of the Cup. The occasion never arose for Chelsea went all the way to Wembley and beat Leeds in the final.

LOYAL HAMMERS

West Ham have had only eight managers in their 98-year history – Syd King, Charlie Paynter, Ted Fenton, Ron Greenwood, John Lyall, Lou Macari, Billy Bonds and Harry Redknapp.

SHOP TILL YOU DROP

In 1998 Swindon Town manager Jimmy Quinn announced that he was banning his players from supermarket shopping in the three days before a match. Quinn explained: "Trailing round the shops with your missus for three hours can wear you out. I don't want them lugging heavy bags of shopping around."

IN GOOD NICK

In Bill Nicholson's first game as Spurs manager, on 11 October 1958, his new team crushed Everton 10–4.

REVOLVING DOORS

Tommy Docherty managed three clubs within the space of six weeks in 1968. He left Rotherham United for Queens Park Rangers in November, but lasted just 28 days at Loftus Road. Shortly afterwards, he took over at Aston Villa. As the Doc himself used to say: "I've had more clubs than Jack Nicklaus!"

YOUNGEST MANAGER

In January 1997 Aurel Rusu, president of Romanian club Sadcom FC, was so dismayed that his team were languishing in the country's bottom division that he appointed his son Lucian as the new manager. Lucian was just six months old.

CHELSEA DROUGHT

When England hat-trick hero Geoff Hurst became manager of Chelsea, he presided over the club's longest goal drought! Chelsea failed to score in the last nine games of the 1980–1 season.

FIRST CASUALTY

Doncaster Rovers' Sammy Chung became the first managerial casualty of the 1996 season when he was sacked on the morning of the opening match! Others who have lasted just 12 days into a season include Len Richley (Darlington, 1971), Dennis Butler (Port Vale, 1979), Mick Jones (Peterborough United, 1989), Peter Reid (Manchester City, 1993), Alan Ball (Manchester City, 1996) and Kerry Dixon (Doncaster Rovers, 1997).

IN THE SACK

In 1992 the coach of a German club was fired for falling in love with the centre-forward. Roland Eybe, 46-year-old coach from Delmenhorst, became infatuated with

RAPID TURNAROUND

Of current Premiership clubs, Bradford City and Manchester City have had most managers since the war. Both have had 23. But the hottest seat in the Football League is Sheffield United. Neil Warnock is the 29th manager at Bramall Lane since 1945.

FOUR MANAGERS AND A FUNERAL

In the course of the 1994–5 season, Notts County had four sets of managers. Mick Walker was sacked less than six months after taking the club to the brink of the First Division play-offs and his successor, Russell Slade, made way for Howard Kendall early in the New Year. Ten weeks later, appropriately on 1 April, Kendall was sacked in favour of a triumvirate comprising Wayne Jones, Steve Nicol and Dean Thomas. At the end of the various comings and goings, Notts were relegated, having finished bottom of the table.

GONE TO SEED

Peter McWilliam, the Tottenham manager of the early 1920s, was desperate to sign inside-forward Jimmy Seed, the star player with Mid-Rhondda. But the Welsh club knew of Spurs' interest and threatened to lynch McWilliam if he came near their ground. So one afternoon in 1920 McWilliam disguised himself in spectacles and a false beard and crept in unnoticed. He was so impressed that he signed Seed immediately after the game for £350.

MANAGERIAL MERRY-GO-ROUND

Southport had four managers in two weeks in 1983. Having sacked Russ Perkins on a Saturday, Southport tried to persuade John King to take over. King provisionally accepted the post on the Tuesday but changed his mind two days later. The following Sunday, Bob Murphy took on the challenge, only to resign on the Thursday. Finally on the Saturday, exactly a fortnight after Perkins' departure, Alex Gibson became Southport manager. He lasted two months.

ALLY OOPS

Facing an injury crisis, Queen of the South manager Ally MacLeod turned out for the club's reserves in 1991, at the age of 58. What's more, he even scored from the penalty spot against St Mirren although the fairy tale didn't have a happy ending – Queens lost 8–1.

FAST FOOD

Grimsby Town's Italian forward Ivano Bonetti suffered a fractured cheekbone in March 1996 after manager Brian Laws allegedly threw a plate of food across the dressing-room following a 3–2 defeat at Luton.

LONG SERVICE

Fred Everiss holds the record as the longest-serving manager at one Football League club. He was in charge at West Bromwich Albion between 1902 and 1948 – a total of 46 years. The longest-serving post-war manager is Sir Matt Busby who reigned supreme at Manchester United for 26 years between 1945 and 1971.

CAME WITH THE SACK

When Joe Royle became manager of Oldham Athletic in 1982, he arrived for his first day in charge in the cab of a coal lorry. He had been forced to hitch a lift after his Jaguar had broken down on the way to Boundary Park.

MAY DAYS

Eddie May had two spells as manager of Cardiff City in 1994–5. He was sacked by the board on 20 November but, following the resignation of his successor, Terry Yorath, May was reappointed on 31 March. But it was too late to save City from relegation.

PLAYING SAFE

Brazil manager Vicente Feola was so worried about the reception he would get back home following his country's early elimination from the 1966 World Cup that he stayed on in England for another month to wait until the dust had settled.

CLOUGH HITS OUT

When celebrating fans ran on to the City Ground pitch

following Nottingham Forest's 5–2 League Cup victory over Queens Park Rangers in 1989, manager Brian Clough reacted by grabbing two fans, clipping them round the ear and dragging them off the playing surface. He later apologised to the pair.

APRIL FOOL

A few minutes after Notts County boss Neil Warnock had handed in his team sheet to referee Terry Lunt before a game at Bristol City in 1991, Lunt realised that the names on it were those of the current England team. Then he remembered the date: 1 April.

21

FAMILY AFFAIRS

LIKE FATHER, LIKE SON

Peter Boyle and Harold Johnson were both members of
the FA Cup-winning Sheffield United teams of 1899
and 1902. And their sons – Thomas Boyle and Harold
Johnson – went on to win the Cup with United in 1925.

THE GENERATION GAME

There have been two occasions at which father and son
have appeared in the same Football League side. Alec
and David Herd played for Stockport County at Hartlepool in a Third Division (North) match on 5 May 1951,
and Ian and Gary Bowyer turned out for Hereford
United against Scunthorpe in a Fourth Division game
on 21 April 1990.

BROTHERS-IN-ARMS

A number of brothers (the latest being Gary and Phil

Neville of Manchester United) have appeared in the same FA Cup Final team, but the only occasion when brothers have been on the opposing side in a final was back in 1874. Herbert Rawson played for the Royal Engineers while his brother William was a member of the victorious Oxford University team.

VARYING FORTUNES

Jack and Bobby Charlton went into management within a few days of each other at the end of the 1973 season, with Middlesbrough and Preston North End respectively. Twelve months later, Jack was leading Middlesbrough to promotion while Bobby had presided over Preston's relegation to Division Three. Incidentally, the Charlton brothers are nephews of Newcastle United legend Jackie Milburn.

WEMBLEY COUSINS

The most recent example of cousins playing in an FA Cup Final was in 1987 when Clive and Paul Allen appeared for Spurs. But in the 1931 final the opposing goalkeepers were cousins. Harry Hibbs was in goal for Birmingham City and his cousin, Harold Pearson, was at the other end of the pitch, in goal for West Bromwich Albion. It was Pearson's day as Albion won 2–1.

BROTHERS SENT OFF

Colchester United brothers Tom and Tony English were

both sent off in a Fourth Division game with Crewe on 26 April 1986.

SUBSTITUTE SON

A son replaced his father during an international between Estonia and Iceland in Tallin on 24 April 1996.
Thirty-five-year-old Arnor Gudjohnsen started the
match for Iceland but was substituted after 62 minutes
to make way for his 17-year-old son Eidur.

THE ALLEN FAMILY

When Bradley Allen made his debut for Queens Park
Rangers in 1989, he was the sixth member of the Allen
family to play League football. He was following in the
footsteps of father Les, a member of the Spurs' double
side of 1960–1, uncle Dennis (who played for Charlton, Reading and Bournemouth), brother Clive, Britain's first £1 million teenager, and cousins Paul and
Martin, both of whom played for a variety of London
clubs.

SAME-NAME MANAGERS

Bill Dodgin Snr and his son, Bill Dodgin Jnr, both had
spells as manager at Fulham. Bill Snr was in charge from
1949 to 1953 while Bill Jnr took over from Bobby

Robson in 1969 and remained in the Craven Cottage hot seat until 1972.

EVER-PRESENT

In the 1970–1 season, brothers Frank, Dave and Bob Worthington were each League ever-presents for their respective clubs – Huddersfield Town, Grimsby Town and Notts County.

TAYLOR-MADE

Brothers Jack and Frank Taylor were full-back partners with Wolves before the Second World War. In June 1952, within a week of each other, both entered football management for the first time – Jack at Queens Park Rangers, Frank at Stoke City. During season 1960–1, they both lost their jobs – Jack at Leeds United, Frank at Stoke.

BARNES STORMERS

Ken and Peter Barnes are the only father and son pairing to score hat-tricks in Division One. Ken netted a hat-trick of penalties for Manchester City against Everton on 7 December 1957 and Peter scored three for West Bromwich Albion against Bolton on 18 March 1980.

MY THREE SONS

Plymouth Argyle manager Bob Jack sold three of his sons to Bolton Wanderers in the 1920s – David (who later became Britain's first £10,000 footballer when he moved to Arsenal in 1928), Robert and Rollo.

THE BROTHERS ATKINSON

Ron Atkinson (nicknamed "The Tank") and his younger brother Graham were key members of the Oxford United team of the 1960s.

KEEPING IT IN THE FAMILY

Brothers Alan and Gary Kelly were the opposing goal-keepers during a Third Division match between Bury and Preston on 13 January 1990. Alan kept goal for Bury while Gary stood between the posts for Preston, the club their father, Alan (senior), played for in the 1964 FA Cup Final.

SHILTON AND SON

In 1994, father and son Peter and Sam Shilton held the records for the oldest and youngest players to appear in a first-team game for Plymouth Argyle. As the club's manager, Peter Shilton picked himself to play against

Burnley in 1993 at the age of 44 and the following year he sent 16-year-old Sam on as an 89th-minute substitute in an FA Cup tie against Bournemouth.

TWIN STRIKERS

When Swindon Town beat Exeter City 2–0 in a Third Division (South) match in 1946–7, their scorers were twins Alf and Bill Stephens.

REPRESENTED DIFFERENT COUNTRIES

John Hollins and his brother Dave won caps for different countries. Midfielder John won one England cap in 1967 while Dave kept goal for Wales on 11 occasions between 1962 and 1966. Ironically Englishman John is now a manager in Wales – with Swansea City.

SON ROSE TO THE OCCASION

For the first time in the history of the FA Cup, a father and son found themselves on opposite sides, during a first qualifying round tie in September 1996. Twenty-year-old Nick Scaife lined up in the Bishop Auckland midfield opposite his 41-year-old father Bobby who played for Pickering. Youth prevailed as Bishops won 3–1.

TWO PAIRS OF BROTHERS

Among the Welsh team that faced Northern Ireland in Belfast on 20 April 1955 were two sets of brothers – Ivor and Len Allchurch and John and Mel Charles.

SIBLING SAINTS

The Southampton side which faced Sheffield Wednesday in a First Division match on 22 October 1988 contained three Wallace brothers – Danny (24) and his 19-year-old twin brothers, Rodney and Ray.

22

NON-LEAGUE

DOVER'S BEEF

Woking's Conference fixture with Dover in April 1995 was called off after the Dover team coach had been held up on the motorway for hours by a stray cow.

CONSOLATION PRIZE

Barton Athletic, beaten in all 26 matches in the Darlington and District League, were surprised to find that at the end of their dismal 1992–3 season, they had won a trophy – the League's fair-play award.

AN OLD HEAD

With his team trailing 8–1 to Bridgwater Town in a Screwfix Direct Western League match in 1998, 53-year-old Calne Town manager Mel Gingell decided to shore up the midfield for the last 20 minutes by bringing on . . . himself. And the move worked. Playing alongside his 15-year-old son Craig, Gingell tightened things up to such an extent that Bridgwater were unable to add to their tally.

TONGUE-TWISTER

A result to tax the *Grandstand* videprinter was the third round Welsh Cup tie in 1986 between Kidderminster Harriers and the Anglesey village with the 58-letter name, usually shortened to Llanfair pg. Ray Mercer, the Kidderminster secretary, who reported the club's matches for local radio, said of the visitors: "I shall refer to them simply as the team from Anglesey."

TALK OF THE TOWN

In 1986 Buckingham Town's centre-forward was arrested by police ten minutes before an FA Cup tie, just as the manager was halfway through his team-talk.

BOLT FROM THE BLUE

Anthony Allden, centre-half with Warwickshire team Highgate United, died after being struck by lightning during an FA Amateur Cup tie with Enfield in 1967. Four other players were also struck and had to be treated for shock.

THREE-TIMES WINNERS

Scarborough and Woking have both won the FA Challenge Trophy three times in a decade. Scarborough won three times in the Seventies (against Wigan Athletic in 1971, Stafford Rangers in 1976 and Dagenham in 1977) while Woking triumphed three times in the Nineties (against Runcorn in 1994, Kidderminster Harriers in 1995 and Dagenham & Redbridge in 1997).

STILL WAITING

At the start of the 1959–60 season, Southern Leaguers Gloucester City recruited the services of 65-year-old Torquay hypnotist Henry Blythe in an attempt to boost their chances of getting into the Football League. They've been playing in a trance ever since.

WEALTHY BENEFACTOR

In 1984, Western Leaguers Wimborne Town, with debts of over £75,000 and attendances below 100, were taken over by an Arab consortium.

THE EXORCIST

Struggling at the foot of the Beazer Homes League in March 1994, Dorchester Town called in the club vicar, Rev. David Fayle, to bless the pitch and remove a curse which had apparently been put on it by a disgruntled supporter, David Green. After the vicar performed the exorcism, Green, a part-time Druid, agreed to lift his spell by chanting in the middle of the pitch. The following day, Dorchester won their first game for months.

STOP THAT MAN (AND HIS DOG)

An opportunist thief ran off with the match ball when it sailed over the Adams Park stand at a 1992 Vauxhall Conference game between Wycombe Wanderers and Yeovil Town. The man was walking his dog but then he quickly tied the animal to a tree, scrambled down an embankment and made off with the £40 ball. Despite being chased by police through surrounding woods, man and dog escaped with the ball using their parked car as a getaway vehicle.

RHYL CONFUSION

Rhyl Athletic had three players called Denis Wilson on their books in the 1956–7 season. They also had two named Billy Hughes.

MOLD Y OLD DOUGH

On her death at the age of 80 in 1979, wealthy widow Katie Williams left one-third of her £123,000 estate to her home-town club, Mold Alexandra of the Welsh National League. That year, Mold were celebrating their 50th anniversary.

MINUS POINTS TOTAL

Dunmow finished the season bottom of the Bishop's Stortford, Stansted and District League Premier Division with minus two points. Not only did they lose all 16 games, conceding 176 goals in the process, but they were also deducted two points for failing to fulfil a fixture.

TOO NARROW

Oxfordshire club Peppard of the Parasol Combined Counties League were thrown out of the 1993 FA Vase because their pitch was too narrow.

IN TUNE

Eager to build a new sports and community centre at their Ryde headquarters, Isle of Wight Saturday Leaguers Oakfield FC applied for £75,000 from National Lottery funds. When the application was refused, the club, reasoning that much of the lottery money appeared to go to the arts, declared itself an operatic society in a bid to obtain a grant. So in 1995, the club's name was officially changed to Oakfield Operatic Society. "Who knows," said manager Mark Cass, "we may find a budding Pavarotti among our ranks."

VISITORS NOT WELCOME

Billingham Synthonia completed their Northern

League fixtures for season 1950–1 without conceding a single goal at home. In reply they scored 44.

WARREN IDEA

Walberswick village football team from Suffolk were given a £1500 council grant in 1992 towards the purchase of a fence to keep burrowing rabbits off the pitch.

CHURCH BLOODBATH

Five players were injured in the annual New Year's Day fixture between the Salvation Army and a church at Sheringham, Norfolk. Baptist minister Mike McGill broke an ankle and two other players suffered broken noses as the 1994 clash turned ugly. McGill confessed: "It was a very rough game and it turned into a bit of a bloodbath." The Salvation Army team won 4–3.

HOAX CALL

In December 1996 a female hoaxer claiming to be a Northern League official tried to get the local derby between Evenwood and Peterlee called off by phoning the referee and two linesmen to tell them that the match was off because of bad weather. But the ruse was discovered when the match officials checked with Evenwood. The referee Paul Thomson said: "I have never come across a situation like this before. We can only guess at why she would want the match called off. It has been suggested that she was a player's wife or girlfriend, but she seemed to be an older lady. Maybe she just hates football.''

THE GROUND OPENED UP

The Vauxhall Conference game between Woking and Hayes on 4 March 1997 was abandoned after 20 minutes when a 3-foot-deep hole suddenly appeared on the pitch at Woking's Kingsfield ground. After Woking skipper Kevan Brown had nearly fallen into it, the referee ruled that it was unsafe for the game to continue.

INSIDE, RIGHT!

After reaching their local cup final, to take place on a neutral ground, prison team Lags XI from Holme House jail in Stockton, Cleveland, were kicked out of the competition because they could only play at home.

23

I DON'T BELIEVE IT!

DEATH WISH

In 1996 a firm of Isle of Wight undertakers – William Hall of Newchurch – announced that they were offering coffins in the deceased's favourite football colours.

FROM PITCH TO PULPIT

In 1997 former Walsall captain Peter Hart announced that he was returning to the town . . . as vicar of St Mary's Church.

DANCING QUEENS

Goal celebrations scaled new heights on Hackney Marshes in February 1997 when Clissold Park Rovers of Thames League Division Three performed an intricate ballet routine to mark a goal in their 2–2 draw with Daz Automatic. Choreographer Kate Brown had been recruited by Rovers to coach the players in more imaginative and artistic ways of expressing their joy at scoring.

CHURCH A-PEAL

Rev. Keith Sinclair was so annoyed about the staging of a Sunday morning game between Aston Villa and Chelsea in March 1999 and the effect that it would have on church attendance that he ordered the bells of his Aston parish church to be rung throughout the televised match.

THE PULL OF THE PLAY-OFFS

The crowd of 73,802 which flocked to Wembley to see Swindon Town defeat Leicester City in the 1993 First Division play-off final was 11,000 bigger than for that year's FA Cup Final replay between Arsenal and Sheffield Wednesday.

THE THREE-HOUR MATCH

A Third Division (North) Cup tie between Stockport County and Doncaster Rovers on 30 March 1946 lasted over three hours. Since it was the second leg, the rules of the competition stated that a golden goal would come into effect if the scores were still level at the end of extra time. But after 203 minutes, neither side had managed to break the deadlock and the players were too exhausted to continue. The match was re-played four days later and Doncaster won 4–0.

FIRST JOBS

Neville Southall used to be a dustman . . . Pat Jennings was a milkman . . . Peter Beardsley made ship valves . . . Kevin Keegan worked as a storeroom clerk . . . Vinnie Jones was a hod carrier . . . Ian Wright used to be a plasterer . . . and Chris Waddle used to work in a factory making the seasoning for sausages.

THE LURE OF WREXHAM RESERVES

A crowd of 18,069 turned up for a reserve match between Wrexham and Winsford United in 1957 after the Welsh club announced that tickets would be on sale for the forthcoming FA Cup tie with Manchester United.

NEVILLE NEVILLE

Phil and Gary Neville's father is called Neville.

VERY SUPERSTITIOUS

Southend United midfielder Phil Gridelet was highly superstitious and insisted on always being the last player to come out on to the pitch at the start of each half. But when United met Ipswich in 1997, Gridelet's team-mate Andy Rammell had trouble with his contact lenses at half-time, delaying his exit from the dressing-room. But Gridelet steadfastly remained there too so that he could be the last to leave. As a result, Southend kicked off the second half with only nine men. Manager Ronnie Whelan labelled Gridelet's decision "crazy".

THE LONG AND SHORT OF IT

Among Lincoln City's playing staff for season 1958–9 was a 6 foot 3 inch centre-half called Ray Long and a 5 foot 2 inch left-winger named Ray Short.

WHAT A PLONKER!

Blackpool midfielder Gary Brabin was fined two weeks' wages in 1998 for placing a condom on a team-mate's shoulder during a team photo. Brabin draped the sheath over Martin Bryan during a pre-season shoot, but was horrified to see the picture printed in the local paper.

IDENTICAL TALLY

A total of 1195 goals were scored in the Premier League in 1993–4. And exactly the same number were scored the following season!

DUCKING AND DIVING

Everton and Manchester United Reserves were attacked by a demented duck during a 1996 Pontin's League game at Goodison Park. The bird flew into the United net and pecked their keeper Nick Culkin. In the end United defender Pat McGibbon grabbed the intruder by the throat and handed it to a steward.

LEFT IN THE DARK

Celtic fans who sat down to watch TV highlights of their team's 7–1 thrashing of Rangers in the 1957 Scottish League Cup Final were dismayed that only the first half was shown. The problem was caused by a forgetful cameraman who had omitted to remove the lens cap after the half-time break.

QUITE REMARKABLE

David Coleman once played for Stockport County Reserves. In his days as a young journalist in Cheshire,

Coleman went along to cover a reserve team game at Edgeley Park, only to discover that County were a man short. An accomplished miler, he was asked to make up the numbers.

FAT CHANCE!

In 1998, bookmakers William Hill offered readers of the Brentford fanzine *Thorne in the Side* 1000–1 against Posh Spice marrying the Bees' 31-year-old roly-poly forward Warren Aspinall.

LOST IN THE POST

The Third Division match between Blackburn Rovers and Chesterfield on Boxing Day 1972 had to be replayed because Chesterfield unwittingly fielded an ineligible player. Goalkeeper Jim Brown had been transferred to them on 22 December but the official registration letter to the Football League had been delayed in the Christmas post.

KEEPER COLLIDED WITH CAR

Bernie Marsh, goalkeeper with Balcombe Reserves from the Mid Sussex League, was fouled by a Ford Sierra during a match with Hartfield in 1992–3. With five minutes to go and the ball near the halfway line, a spectator decided to reverse his car on to the pitch in readiness to leave. This manoeuvre coincided with a high lob being delivered towards the Balcombe goal.

Without looking behind him, Marsh ran back and just managed to tip the ball over the bar, but his momentum sent him crashing head first into the car, knocking him out cold. Recovering from his ordeal, he vowed to be extra vigilant in case future opponents sent up the People Carrier for corners.

A SHARED OWN GOAL

Chelsea's second goal in their 3–1 victory over Leicester City on 18 December 1954 produced soccer's only instance of a shared own goal. Two Leicester defenders – Stan Milburn and Jack Froggatt – lunged at the ball in an attempt to clear and connected simultaneously to send it flying into their own net.

THE REAL RON MANAGER

The Fast Show's Ron Manager is based on former Queens Park Rangers boss Alec Stock who guided the then Third Division club to League Cup success in 1967. Stock once bought the entire Rangers team pork-pie hats like his own as a reward for winning a vital promotion match.

CELEBRITY FOOTBALLERS

Chat show host Des O'Connor was a nippy winger with Northampton Town just after the war; Angus Deayton once had trials with Crystal Palace; 16-year-old Rod Stewart was an apprentice with Brentford for three weeks; and former *It's a Knockout* host Stuart Hall played for Crystal Palace Reserves in 1953.

LINCOLN: BEHIND CLOSED DOORS

During the First World War, soccer was considered to be a threat to national security. Questions were raised in the House of Commons after a number of British-made shells had failed to explode in France. It was decided that those making the shells must have been distracted and so no football matches were allowed to take place near munitions factories during working hours. So in 1915 an FA Cup second replay between Bradford City and Norwich, at Lincoln, was staged behind closed doors.

POOCH POUNCES

One of the scorers in a Staffordshire Sunday Cup tie between Knave of Clubs and Newcastle Town went down in the record books as A. Dog. Knave of Clubs were 2–0 down when one of their forwards broke clear on goal. His mis-hit shot was going harmlessly wide until a mongrel dog ran on to the pitch, jumped up at the bouncing ball and headed it past the Newcastle keeper and into the net. Despite Newcastle protests, the referee gave the goal. Newcastle held on to win 3–2.

ENGLISH TAKEAWAY

The replay for the 1934 Welsh Cup Final was fought out

Anja Bresch, 23, the star striker with the women's team. He got the boot after his wife walked out and half of the players quit because he spent so little time trying to improve the side's miserable record.

HOLLAND'S DOUBLE DUTCH

Despite having 125 England caps and over 1000 League games to his name, Peter Shilton was sacked by Leyton Orient manager Pat Holland in 1997 because he couldn't kick the ball far enough.

A MAN FOR ALL SEASONS

Tony Parkes has stepped in as caretaker-manager of Blackburn Rovers on no fewer than five occasions.

CUP WINNERS AT THE BRIDGE

In the 1990s, Chelsea had three successive managers, each of whom had scored the winning goal in an FA Cup Final – Ian Porterfield (for Sunderland, 1973), David Webb (for Chelsea, 1970) and Glenn Hoddle (for Spurs, 1982).

DOUBLE TROUBLE

John Bond, Ron Saunders, Bob Stokoe, Billy McNeill, Dave Bassett and Mick Mills all had the misfortune to manage two clubs that were relegated in the same season. In 1985–6, Bond had spells at Swansea City and Birmingham City, both of whom went down at the end of the season. His predecessor at St Andrews was Ron Saunders who, in that same year, was in charge of the West Brom team which finished bottom of the First Division. In 1986–7, Billy McNeill was in charge of first Manchester City and then Aston Villa, both of whom were relegated from the First Division at the end of the campaign. And Bob Stokoe also suffered a double relegation that year with Carlisle United and Sunderland. The following season saw Dave Bassett leave Watford, who were eventually relegated to Division Two, and take over at Sheffield United, who plunged down to Division Three. Then in 1989–90, Mick Mills failed to work his magic at either Stoke City or Colchester United.

TOSHACK'S BRIEF REIGN

John Toshack had just once game in charge of Wales in 1994 – a 3–1 defeat to Norway at Ninian Park – before resigning after 48 days at the helm.

GET SMART

Middlesbrough manager John Neal ordered winger Terry Cochrane to improve his appearance on the field in 1980 after Cochrane wore his shirt outside his shorts and had his socks rolled down when he came on as substitute in a pre-season friendly against a Yugoslavian team.

between two English teams on an English ground!
Bristol City met Tranmere Rovers at Chester's Sealand
Road. City won 3–0 and the cup stayed in English
hands until 1948.

A COOL HEAD

Full-back Jock Drummond, who joined Rangers from
Falkirk in 1892, used to wear a cloth cap during matches
to keep cool.

BACK FROM THE DEAD

In 1993, players and supporters of HFS Loans League
team Congleton were forced to call off a minute's
silence to mourn the death of the club's oldest
fan . . . when he turned up at the ground. Die-hard
supporter Fred Cope, aged 85, arrived at the Cheshire
club's ground for the fixture with Rossendale to find
the flag flying at half-mast. He assumed it was as a
tribute to Bobby Moore, who had died that week, but
when he started to read the match-day programme, he
was horrified to see that it contained his own obituary,
complete with a photograph. So as the players and
referee lined up on the pitch to pay their last respects,
Fred thought that he had better point out to officials
that rumours regarding his death were greatly exagger-
ated. The confusion arose after another fan had inno-
cently spread the news that Fred had died. "We took
him at his word," said Congleton manager Bill Wright,
"and thought it would be nice to give Fred a tribute as

he is so popular. It was a shock when he turned up!" To underline his well-being, Fred went on to win a bottle of whisky in the half-time raffle.

CORNER COUNT

Nottingham Forest forced 22 corners as opposed to Southampton's two during a Premiership game in November 1992. Yet Saints won 2–1. Even more hard done by were Sheffield United against West Ham in October 1989. United forced 28 corners to West Ham's one but still lost 2–0.

PLAYED A BLINDER!

Montrose collected their first major trophy in their 106-year existence by winning the Second Division Championship in 1985 ... despite having a goalkeeper named Ray Charles.

WITCH DOCTOR HIRED

At its annual meeting in 1957, the Salisbury and District Football Association of Rhodesia formally approved the payment of £10 for the services of a witch doctor. Salisbury had lost every one of their matches the previous season.

THE NEW BROOM

When Tom Whittaker took charge of Arsenal at the start of the 1947–8 season, he immediately guided the Gunners to a run of 17 unbeaten matches in the League.

ONE MAN WENT TO MOW

In his days as manager at Barnet, Barry Fry was once spotted by police mowing the Underhill pitch by moonlight at four o'clock on a Saturday morning. He explained to the officers that he was so worked up about that afternoon's match that he hadn't been able to sleep and had decided to do something useful instead.

FELL OFF ROOF

Former Oldham Athletic manager David Ashworth used to watch the game from the flat roof of the stand at Boundary Park, running up and down to keep up with play. But one day he got so carried away he fell over the edge and had to be dragged back up by Latics' supporters.

CUP DOUBLES

The only managers to have won the FA Cup with

different clubs are Herbert Chapman (Huddersfield Town, 1922, and Arsenal, 1930) and Billy Walker (Sheffield Wednesday, 1935, and Nottingham Forest, 1959).

PLAY-OFF SPECIALIST

When Plymouth Argyle won promotion to the Second Division in 1996, it was manager Neil Warnock's fourth play-off success in seven seasons, following on from two with Notts County and one with Huddersfield Town.

SEND IN THE CLOWNS

Beleaguered Spurs manager Christian Gross announced plans to take the players to the circus in January 1998 in an effort to boost morale.

LOVE HURTS

Six weeks after leading Manchester United to their 1977 FA Cup triumph, Tommy Docherty was sacked as manager for announcing that he was leaving his wife and four children to live with Mary Brown, wife of United physio Laurie Brown. United insisted that Docherty had been sacked for transgressing the club's "moral code". The Doc said: "I have been punished for falling in love."

A SPATE OF BURST BALLS

On the evening before the 1946 FA Cup Final between Derby County and Charlton, the referee was asked by the BBC what the chances were of the ball bursting. He confidently stated that the odds against that happening were about a million to one. Yet the following day the ball did burst for the first time in an FA Cup Final. And when the two clubs met in a League match five days later, the ball burst again! The story doesn't even end there because the following year Charlton were back at Wembley to face Burnley and, believe it or not, the ball burst once more. The reason given for these freakish incidents was that immediately after the war, the balls were made of inferior leather.

DELAYED FINISH

When the match between Sheffield Wednesday and Aston Villa in November 1898 was abandoned through bad light after 79½ minutes, the two teams were ordered to reconvene four months later to play the remaining ten and a half minutes. In that time, Wednesday added a fourth goal to run out 4–1 winners.

VALUABLE BOOTY

Thieves stole 175 pairs of football boots from Everton's training ground in 1977.

MISTAKEN IDENTITY

Acting on an anonymous tip-off that a cannabis plant was growing in the club reception area, police officers swooped on the offices of Northampton Town in August 1997. They left clutching a sprig of plastic weeping fig.

MADE AN EXHIBITION OF HIMSELF

For a 1977 exhibition, artist Philip Core constructed life-size figures of the entire Queens Park Rangers team from half-inch-thick plywood. After receiving admiring glances travelling on the London Underground with his wooden Stan Bowles, Core declared his intention to add the Watford team, two policemen, a referee and linesman and a streaker.

THE BITER BIT

A police dog had part of its ear bitten off during trouble at the West Ham–Arsenal match on 8 April 1987. One man was also treated for dog bite.

ARREST THAT MAN

When the Killingbeck police side discussed at half-time

how they could save a vital Leeds Floodlit League match from 2–0 down, one of the players suddenly realised that the St Nicholas number 11, who had been running them ragged, was on the wanted list. A phone call was quickly made to colleagues at the station and within a few minutes the opposition danger man was under arrest. St Nicholas had no substitute available, allowing the police team to launch a spirited fight back and boost their title chances with a 6–3 win. League secretary Malcolm Cuthbert said: "Officers from Killingbeck police station arrived at the ground just after the start of the second half and hauled the player off, still wearing his kit. There's nothing in the rules to stop a police side arresting one of the opposition players if they are wanted for a crime, but I suppose it does rather give police teams an unfair advantage."

KICKING UP A STINK

In August 1997, Bury players announced that they were refusing to do any more promotional work for the club in protest at the lack of nappy-changing facilities for their wives at Gigg Lane.

BLACKADDER GOES NORTH

Among Carlisle United's playing staff for 1946–7 was centre-half Fred Blackadder.

GIRLS IN BRAWL

In 1982 police were called in to break up a fight at a girls' five-a-side tournament between two Croydon schools. The tournament had been organised by the Metropolitan Police.